50

□ MURDEROUS PLACES □

MURDEROUS PLACES

Michael Prince

BLANDFORD

First published in the UK 1989 by **Blandford Press**,
An imprint of Cassell,
Artillery House, Artillery Row, London SW1P 1RT

Distributed in the United States by
Sterling Publishing Co., Inc.,
2 Park Avenue, New York, NY 10016

Distributed in Australia by
Capricorn Link (Australia) Pty Ltd,
PO Box 665, Lane Cove, NSW 2066

British Library Cataloguing in Publication Data
Prince, Michael
  Murderous places
  1. Great Britain. Places associated with murder
  I. Title
  914.1'504852

ISBN 0-7137-2007-7

Typeset by St George Typesetting, Redruth, Cornwall

Printed in Great Britain by Mackays of Chatham

Contents

1

□□■□□

Room 4

■ EVERY day hundreds of people unwittingly follow in the footsteps of evil. Unknowingly, they sleep in a room where a particularly heinous murder was committed, or admire the serenity at the scene of a massacre, or enjoy a picnic at a beauty spot that was once a killer's playground.

But when one returns knowingly to 'Murderous Places', the horror of the original event that inspired your macabre pilgrimage can be overwhelming.

So it was with me as I climbed six well-scrubbed stone steps from the uneven pavement to the quiet entrance to Pembridge Court Hotel in London's cosmopolitan Notting Hill Gate.

Pedestrians in Pembridge Gardens passed me by without a second glance as I paused in the Victorian porch under a gently oscillating lantern-light, which creaked eerily as it was buffeted by a night wind.

Neville George Clevely Heath must have stood on the very same spot as he let himself into the Hotel with his night key, just after midnight on the morning of Friday, June 21, 1946. Beside him was Margery Aimee Brownell Gardner, who earned a modest living as a film extra. When she was out of work, she was never short of handsome escorts to take care of her needs.

Margery Gardner, at thirty-two, was most attractive to men. She was the sort of woman no man would forget. The taxi driver who had driven them from the Panama Club in South Kensington could not take his eyes off her as, giggling, full of

7

life and vivacity, she tottered up the steps, slightly the worse for drink, a slender arm around the waist of her debonair companion.

They looked the perfect couple: the beautiful princess with her tall and dashing Prince Charming. However, the casual observer would have been wrong to assume that they were deeply in love. Neither were as they seemed. Both, in their different ways, were phony. He was known to her as Lieutenant-Colonel Heath: at least he was consistent with his lie that month, having prefaced his name with high military rank in the hotel register. Margery's fresh air of innocence was deceptive. She had a husband from whom she was separated, and bed-hopping was her major enthusiasm. Her extensive wardrobe of clothes, including all her French underwear, had been acquired as gifts from the entourage of admirers whom she actively encouraged. 'Flighty', was how she was described by her contemporaries in the British film industry. 'She's the underlay of the casting-couch,' sneered her bitchy rivals.

Poised between the two white pillars, they must have heard the taxi's engine ticking over, before the gear grated and a frustrated, envious cabbie headed west towards the bright lights, unaware that he was soon to be a key witness in one of Britain's most infamous murder cases.

In the small foyer, Heath and Mrs Gardner would have passed on their right the same small, unmanned reception desk at which I hesitated. Keys hang on hooks. There are glossy pamphlets in racks. An inner, closet-sized room accommodates the switchboard.

The hotel has always been privately owned. Originally, it was a gracious nineteenth-century private house, during which time downstairs folk attended to the demands of the gentry upstairs. Horse-drawn carriages and gas lamps graced the surrounding squares and crescents. The white walls and black railings have survived the ravages of time.

On the way to the stairs, which face the entrance, I passed under another lantern. The ceiling is high and as a result voices become lofty. Room 4 is on the first floor at the back, overlooking small gardens and Pembridge Road. It is one of the most spacious of the twenty-six rooms in the hotel: Victorian prints adorn the pastel walls; flowery drapes are held apart during the day by matching sashes; there is a private bathroom, direct-dial telephone, colour television, radio and hair-dryer. However, it was rather different in 1946. The hotel has changed hands since then, and only after 1977 was it 'sympathetically' modernized. The façade is still as Victorian in style as the day it was built.

In the early hours of the morning of June 21, 1946, Neville Heath and Margery Gardner would have been making the most of more Spartan surroundings: twin beds, worn carpet, no bathroom, fading curtains and a gas fire.

In those days, Pembridge Court Hotel catered mainly for people who had been comfortably off, but for whom money was now tighter — hence the number of retired army officers and widows of military gentlemen peppered through the register. However, neither Heath nor Mrs Gardner was there for the facilities.

It was around 2 a.m. of the same morning that Heath left the hotel. As he slammed the bedroom door, he disturbed the occupant of the next room, who looked at his bedside alarm clock before turning over and returning to sleep. Suddenly, Heath was alone. A lot had happened during the hour-and-three-quarters that he and Mrs Gardner had been together in Room 4.

As Heath descended the stone steps to Pembridge Gardens, by that time of night a sleepy backwater, he must have been wondering which way to run. A left turn within a hundred yards would have taken him into the Portobello Road, world-famous for its antiques market. More seductive, though, were the come-hither smiles of Notting Hill Gate and the busy Bayswater Road, just a brisk two-minute walk to his right, where taxis maundered up and down during the night. Within five minutes, he was on his way west.

The chambermaid first knocked on the door of Room 4 at 9 a.m. When there was no answer, she went away, continuing her daily chores elsewhere, and returned an hour later. Still there was no reply and the door was locked. She tried two more times before she gave up, exasperated, and went for lunch at noon.

When she had no luck at 2 p.m., the chambermaid fetched the assistant manageress, who unlocked the door with the master key and ventured in. The room was too dim to see much. Instead of switching on the light, she crossed the room and drew back the curtains. Then she turned to examine the room, particularly the twin beds.

The bed near the window had not been slept in, but the one by the door was in disarray. The shape of the heaped bedclothes indicated that someone was still in the bed.

Politely, the assistant manageress coughed, hoping to wake the sleeping guest whom she knew to be the charming Lieutenant-Colonel Heath, without too much embarrassment. 'Excuse me, sir, are you all right? I'm afraid the chambermaid will be going off duty shortly and...'. She cut herself short, realizing that all was not well. Gathering herself, she strode purposefully to the occupied bed and tentatively peeled back the covers, then retreated in wide-eyed disbelief, her hands clasped to her mouth, while the chambermaid ran screaming hysterically from the room and down the stairs.

The woman's naked body was face downwards, her ankles tied together and arms folded behind her back. The victim was, of course, Margery Gardner.

The case was assigned to Scotland Yard's Detective Chief Inspector Thomas Barratt. From the hotel, Barratt put out a call for Professor Keith Simpson, who had become the first Professor of Forensic Medicine at London University. Simpson was tracked down to the Detective Training College in Hendon where he was lecturing, whilst his secretary, Jean Scott-Dunn, whom he was later to marry, was found under a hairdryer in Knightsbridge. They met at 6.30 p.m. at the foot of the bed in Room 4 of the Pembridge Court Hotel. They first noticed seventeen whiplash weals across the victim's body. Both nipples of her breasts had been bitten off and there were other bite marks on the body. An internal examination revealed a seven-inch-long rent in the vagina, plus internal injuries. Bleeding had been profuse.

Simpson knew instantly that sexual intercourse could not possibly have been responsible for the internal injuries, and he informed Barratt of this.

Lying in the fireplace was a short, stocky poker, which Simpson confirmed 'could possibly' have been the weapon which was used.

Naturally, Barratt was eager to establish the cause of death as quickly as possible. The absence of head injuries ruled out battering and the extensive internal bleeding indicated that Mrs Gardner had been alive, if not fully conscious, when violated by the poker, or similar instrument. Professor Simpson noted the blue hue of her face and informed Barratt that all the signs suggested that Mrs Gardner had died from asphyxia — although, of course, this was only a preliminary assessment.

The body was removed to the Hammersmith Mortuary, where Professor Simpson conducted a post-mortem, confirming his initial opinion through the discovery of 'typical asphyxial changes in the heart and lungs'. The lack of strangulation marks meant that the cause of death *had* to be suffocation and this conclusion was immediately communicated to Barratt, whose forensic team was still beavering for clues at the hotel.

When someone dies of asphyxiation, there is a rise in body temperature: Professor Simpson made allowances for that when calculating the time of death, which he put at 'not before midnight and no later than the earliest hours of the morning'. He was, of course, correct.

All residents and members of staff at the Pembridge Court Hotel were interviewed. Barratt was satisfied that the witness who testified to hearing a door slam at 2 a.m. had pinpointed the exact time of Heath's departure. Later, a taxi driver was to describe to the inspector how he picked up a couple outside the Panama Club and drove them to the Pembridge Court Hotel, arriving at 12.15 a.m. or 'thereabouts'. He would never forget the woman, he said, and promptly identified Margery Gardner from a publicity photograph. The victim's estranged husband was traced and quickly eliminated from suspicion.

The killer had not made any attempt to conceal the woman's identity: her personal belongings, including driving licence, cheque book, purse and letters were found in a handbag on a chair. Something else puzzled Barratt: why had no one heard any screams? Mrs Gardner had been brutally thrashed, yet the person next door had heard nothing, except a door being closed rather clumsily. Mrs Gardner had been bound and probably gagged: slight flushes around her wrists and lips suggested to Professor Simpson that her hands, as well as her feet, had been tied and something like a scarf had been tightened over her mouth. But why was there no evidence of a struggle? Why had she gone, apparently, so passively and mutely to her death?

The fingerprint scientists had a lot to keep them occupied as Heath's dabs were all over the bedroom, including the poker. The prints were matched with those on a Scotland Yard file on Neville George Clevely Heath, and Barratt soon realized that he was looking for a man who was no stranger to the police.

Years later, a Mrs Heather Bride was staying with her eleven-year-old daughter at the Pembridge Court Hotel. They were on a two-week touring vacation from Chicago, Illinois: Mr Bride had remained at home to look after their two much younger children.

At around 1.50 a.m., on the second day of their holiday, Mrs Bride shot up screaming in her twin bed — the one near the door — clutching her back. 'Someone hit me!' she shouted. 'There's someone in the room! Who hit me?'

Her daughter, Lisa, jumped from her bed and switched on the light. The door was bolted from the inside. The window was locked, the latch securely in place. There was no one under either bed, nor in the wardrobe.

Mrs Bride was still shaking with fright, and when she lowered her nightdress, Lisa was able to see the three fresh whiplash-looking weals on her mother's back!

The date was June 21, 1956, the tenth anniversary of Margery Gardner's death. The room was No. 4, and the bed in which Mrs Bride had been sleeping was that on which Mrs Gardner had died.

Heath was born in 1917 in Ilford, Essex, and was educated first at a Catholic primary school and later at the local grammar school. A violent streak manifested itself while he was still only a young boy, when, for no apparent reason except self-gratification, he flogged a little girl at school so severely that she had to be taken home by car and put to bed. The girl's parents declined to press charges against Heath, in order to spare their daughter an even more traumatic ordeal in court.

By the age of thirteen, Heath was a regular pipe-smoker and already dating girls several years older than himself. He was only fifteen when he had a sexual relationship, lasting for several months, with the mother of a boy in one of the junior classes at his grammar school. Despite his outrageous behaviour in adolescence, he survived his school days without suspension or expulsion, leaving at the age of seventeen, without a career in mind.

For two years, he remained unemployed, until successfully applying for a short-service commission in the RAF, only to be court-martialled a year later for stealing a car from an NCO, going AWOL (Absent Without Leave) and absconding from a Military Police detention centre. He was convicted on all charges and expelled from the Service with a dishonourable discharge.

The women who were mesmerized by Heath's charisma considered him to be intelligent, but this was not the case; he never learned from his mistakes. For example, in November, 1937, no more than two months after he was discharged in disgrace from the RAF, he posed as a 'Lord Dudley', once again stole cars, and fraudulently obtained credit at an hotel in Nottingham.

When he was arrested, he was asked: 'Are you Lord Dudley?'

His answer was predictable. 'I *am*, old man.'

To which the police officer countered laconically: 'And I'm Detective Inspector Hickman of the Nottingham CID.'

Unperturbed, Heath accepted his fate promptly: 'In that case, old man, I am *not* Lord Dudley.'

Life was a game to him and people were his playthings. His extravagant personality accounts for his appeal to women, and whilst he seemed the epitome of the lovable rogue, beneath the charming veneer was a dark side always eager for expression.

Most men who met Heath for the first time were struck by his cruel eyes and the sardonic slant at the edges of his mouth — features of which his many lovers were oblivious. When he appeared in court in Nottingham, he was placed on probation for two years, the magistrates convinced that he was no worse than a 'high-spirited bounder', a potential bulldog Biggles should war with Germany ever take place.

In May the following year, he smooth-talked his way into a salesman's job in Oxford Street, London, only to be dismissed within a fortnight for stealing money from the till. By now he was an habitual criminal, although hardly a professional one. In terms of quality and success, he remained very much an amateur. In July of the same year, 1938, he was back in court to face thirteen charges, ranging from house-breaking to theft. He had even stolen from an ingénue who had become his fiancée after only two meetings.

The women to whom Heath was irresistible did not believe him to be rotten, merely incorrigible. Without exception, they all deluded themselves into believing they could change him. However, the court decided that Borstal was the only hope for Heath, and that is where he stayed until the outbreak of World War II in 1939, when he was released in order that he could be conscripted into the army.

It is hard to imagine that anyone with Heath's record might be considered for the post of officer. However, in March, 1940, he was once again commissioned!

Even during the War he found time for villainy which culminated in yet another court martial and his being cashiered. In addition to going AWOL (he was fortunate that this offence just fell short of desertion), Heath had stolen an army pay book so that he was receiving two salaries.

During the voyage back to Britain on the troopship Mooltan, Heath devised a deadly scheme. When the ship docked at Durban, he promptly fled, assuming the name 'Captain Selway', MC, a hero of the Argyll and Sutherland Highlanders, then he made for Johannesburg under the assumed identity of plain 'Mr Armstrong'. But the police net had already begun to tighten around the fictitious Captain Selway who had a penchant for the High Life, financed, unfortunately, with forged cheques. His nerve knew no bounds. Instead of lying low, he swaggered into the nearest military recruitment centre and joined the South African Air Force. On the enlistment form, the recruitment officer wrote: 'Very personable. Easy conversationalist. A born leader. Most definitely officer material.' Incredibly, it was a matter of only months before Robert Armstrong had risen to the rank of captain with a record-sheet that suggested he could look forward to a top-brass future, if he survived the war. All this was achieved without Robert Armstrong needing to reveal his non-existent past.

Although a rake of considerable aplomb and audacity, Heath was constantly in search of love and security, as his proposals of marriage to every girl dated more than once would indicate. This contradiction in his character pointed to powerful emotional conflicts within himself. While other men of his age had girlfriends, Heath had fiancées, many of them much younger than himself, such as Elizabeth Pitt, daughter of a wealthy diamond miner. This relationship resulted in marriage, even though Elizabeth was only sixteen years old. While Elizabeth was bearing him a son, he reverted to his old ways. The day he almost drowned a girl in a swimming pool by holding her under the water until she became unconscious was a portent that went unheeded. In his usual convincing style, he persuaded everyone that the near-tragedy had been an accident, an act of playful folly — despite the fact that the girl was clinically dead when lifted from the water, and survived only because an expert in artificial respiration happened to be at the poolside.

Still using the name Armstrong, Heath was loaned in February, 1944, to the RAF, no one suspecting that he was the same reprobate who had already been thrown out of both the RAF and the British Army. However, some of his luck ran out during his first flight with 180 Squadron. He was shot down over enemy territory, although he managed to bale out in time to save his life. When captured by the Germans, he co-operated and collaborated to ensure that he sat out the rest of the war without too much loss of comfort.

By the time the war was over 'Mrs Armstrong' was already well into divorce proceedings against her husband for desertion. On Heath's return to South Africa, he pleaded with his wife to change her mind, but she was adamant and in October, 1945, the marriage was officially dissolved. This prompted Heath to embark on yet another crime spree, resulting in his being dismissed from the South African Air Force.

Without a future in South Africa, Heath returned to Britain in February, 1946, and reverted to his real name — apart from those occasions when it suited him to be accepted as a peer of the realm or a top-ranking military officer. Nothing had changed. He had been home scarcely two months when he was fined £10 by Wimbledon magistrates for 'illegally wearing military uniforms and decorations'.

It was on Sunday, June 16, 1946, that Heath checked into Room 4 of the Pembridge Court Hotel, giving a false address in Romney. With him was a slim, dark-haired young woman who he introduced as his 'new wife', giving the impression that they had recently married. In fact, they had known one another barely twenty-four hours! The latest woman in his life, Yvonne, was already hoping to become the legitimate Mrs Heath: I shall not identify her because she has been happily married for many years and has a grown-up family and grandchildren who are all probably ignorant of this embarrassing episode in her distant past.

Heath had met Yvonne on the Saturday at a dance in Chelsea, before escorting her home to the Overseas Club, where she had a room. On the Sunday, he took her to the Panama Club, which had become his favourite haunt. They danced and drank until late, then returned to Room 4 of the Pembridge Court Hotel, sleeping together in the very bed on which Margery Gardner was to die so violently five days later. In the morning, they had breakfast together in the hotel, looking to the other guests like the dewy-eyed newly-weds they purported to be. The restaurant was very different then, of course. Nowadays, Caps restaurant in the basement has quite a reputation with discerning diners. Its decor theme of schoolboy caps has made it something of a star attraction in the Notting Hill Gate area — especially among tourists — but in 1946 the restaurant was nothing more elaborate than a modest breakfast room.

Monday morning, Yvonne returned by train to her parents in Worthing, Sussex. Heath promised to telephone her later in the week to make arrangements to meet her family: in fact, he called her more than once between the Monday and Thursday. Yvonne was to tell the police that Heath had been 'very sweet and gentle' when they made love in Room 4 on the Sunday. According to her account, there had been no perversion and nothing sadistic about Heath's behaviour towards her. 'He was very loving and tender towards me from beginning to end,' she told Barratt.

On the morning of the murder, Heath set out for Worthing, although this was not known to the police during their initial inquiries. Barratt had no trouble piecing together Heath's movements *before* the murder, but from 2 a.m. on the Friday, the trail went mysteriously cold.

On reaching Worthing, Heath telephoned Yvonne from the railway station: he had caught the first train of the day from Victoria. They met on the Friday, and on the Saturday Heath was introduced to Yvonne's parents, who were immediately impressed by him, instinctively convinced that he was 'right' for their daughter. Although they were opposed to shotgun weddings, they gave their blessing to Yvonne's rushed marriage plans. However, their attitude changed dramatically the following morning, when they read in the Sunday newspapers that Heath was wanted by Scotland Yard for questioning 'in connection' with the Margery Gardner murder.

Yvonne wasted no time telephoning Heath at his hotel in Worthing (where they had made love on both the Friday and Saturday evenings). 'We've all read the papers,' she told him fretfully. 'My parents are frantic.'

'Yes, I thought they would be,' said Heath, in something of an understatement. 'I'm going to London straight away to sort things out. This is a terrible mistake. I'll ring you tonight.' He did not call that night and Yvonne never heard from him again.

Instead of returning to London, Heath (now in the guise of 'Group Captain Rupert Brooke') headed westwards along the coast to sedate Bournemouth and booked into the Tollard Royal Hotel, an austere, domed building high on the cliff-edge overlooking the sea, just a few hundred yards short of neighbouring Poole. The building is still very much the same as it was then, but no longer an hotel, having been converted into flats during the Fifties, and now bearing the name Tollard Court. Next door is the four-star Highcliff Hotel, where Prime Minister Margaret Thatcher and her Government Cabinet stayed during the 1986 Conservative Party Conference.

Back in London, Professor Simpson had told Inspector Barratt: 'If you find that whip, you've found your man.' The diamond-patterned weals on Margery Gardner's flesh were so vivid and detailed that Simpson was able, in his own words, 'to measure them with mathematical precision'.

Through information from Yvonne and her parents, the police hunt focused on the south coast, though Barratt suspected that Heath had caught a train back to London, hoping to prove the theory that there is safety in numbers. In the meantime, photographs of Heath were circulated to every police station in the United Kingdom. By this time, Barratt was in possession of a letter, posted in Worthing, which had been written to him and signed '*N.G.C. Heath*'.

In the letter, Heath claimed that he had loaned his room at the Pembridge Court Hotel to a man called Jack who wanted to entertain Margery Gardner for a few hours. He said that Mrs Gardner had invited him (Heath) to sleep with her after she had finished with Jack at about 2 a.m. Heath's letter went on:

'It must have been almost 3 a.m. when I returned to the hotel and found her in the condition of which you are aware. I realized that I was in an invidious position, and rather than notify the police, I packed my belongings and left. Since then I have been in several minds whether to come forward or not, but in view of the circumstances I have been afraid to....I have the instrument with which Mrs Gardner was beaten and am forwarding it to you today. You will find my fingerprints on it, but you should also find others as well.'

The whip never arrived.

The room Heath was given at the Tollard Royal Hotel was No. 71, but he soon asked to be moved into a room with a gas fire, which the manager regarded as a very strange request in the month of June. During his stay, Heath wrote a letter on hotel notepaper to his parents, saying: 'Life to me doesn't mean a thing. I intend to end my life.' Is that why he had asked for a room with a gas fire? No one will ever know for certain.

During the morning of Wednesday, July 3, Heath went for a stroll, joining the hundreds of holidaymakers on the promenade. Summer was in the air and colourful clothes and bright smiles decorated the seafront.

Doreen Marshall, a very attractive brunette on holiday from Pinner in Middlesex, was not in the habit of allowing herself to be 'picked-up' by strangers, but she was no match for Heath's glib tongue and suave technique. She was standing near the pier, enjoying the sun and the sea, when Heath made an idle remark to her. Doreen turned to find herself looking at one of the handsomest men she had ever seen. Heath was reclining on the promenade railing, lighting a pipe: he was confident that a pipe enhanced his appeal to women. In fact, Doreen, who had recently celebrated her twenty-first birthday, had once confided in a friend in the WRENS, probably half-jesting, that she 'couldn't resist' pipe-smokers.

Heath and Miss Marshall were still talking an hour after he had moved in for the kill. The pick-up had been so painless, so perfected: within the first couple of sentences, Heath made sure he had divulged the 'fact' that he was a Group Captain in the RAF.

'The name's Rupert Brooke — no relation of the poet chap, I'm afraid!'

'I'm Doreen Marshall,' she said, shaking his hand enthusiastically, apparently adding: 'I like a man with a strong handshake: it means he can be trusted.'

They both laughed.

Doreen was pleased to accept Heath's invitation to join him at his hotel for tea that afternoon. They sat in the crowded lounge with other guests, Doreen in an appropriate summer frock and Heath dressed casually in a check-shirt, without tie, and cavalry trousers. A waitress served tea, cucumber sandwiches and cakes to their table beside a large bay window, which gave them an unimpeded view of the garden and the start of the zig-zag path leading down the cliff to the beach.

Doreen explained that she had only just been demobbed from the WRENS.

'And what brings you to Bournemouth?' asked Heath (always attentive when in the company of women).

Doreen had suffered a particularly severe bout of 'flu and her father, a company director, recommended Bournemouth as the ideal place for convalescence. She had travelled first class from Waterloo on the Bournemouth Belle and was staying alone in one of the best rooms at the Royal Norfolk Hotel.

No doubt, Heath could not believe his luck. When tea was over, he said how much he had enjoyed her company and hoped that they would be able to see one another again very soon. Doreen must have fallen for Heath's plausibility because she was no less eager than he was for a second meeting. Heath proposed a dinner date and seven-fifteen was the time fixed for their next meeting at the Tollard Royal Hotel. Heath hurriedly booked a table for two, informing the head waiter that he would be dining at 8.15.

After dinner, followed by drinks in the lounge, Heath offered to escort Doreen back to the Royal Norfolk Hotel in the town centre, about a mile away. It was midnight when they left the hotel arm-in-arm. The night porter noted the time because Heath said: 'I'll be back in half-an-hour.' The porter, who glanced at the clock, presumed Heath meant 'Don't lock up, I won't be any longer than it takes!'

Anxious not to lock out the debonair Group Captain, the night porter kept his eye, as much as possible, on the main entrance, though his duties took him to other areas of the hotel during the early hours. By 4.30 a.m., as there was still no sign of the hotel's most popular resident, he decided to check Room 81, to which Heath had been assigned on his own request, after expressing his dissatisfaction with Room 71. The bedroom door was unlocked, so the porter peered inside, and with the help of the corridor light he was able to satisfy himself that Heath was indeed in bed and asleep. Beside the bed was a pair of shoes, covered with sand.

The next morning, Heath revealed to the head porter that he had returned to his room at the rear of the hotel during the night via a ladder: 'Just having a bit of sport with your night chappie. All good fun, old chap!'

One or two of the guests commented to one another, knowingly, about the fresh scratches on Heath's neck. In the bar at lunchtime, he overheard the tittering and, as a consequence, no doubt, he appeared at dinner wearing a cravat. Likewise, when he went out 'on the town', his neck and lower face were wrapped in a scarf, despite the warm weather.

The next day, Friday, July 5, Miss Marshall was reported missing to the police by the manager of the Royal Norfolk Hotel. Miss Marshall must have mentioned to someone at the hotel that she was dining with a Group Captain Rupert Brooke at the Tollard Royal, because the manager of the Royal Norfolk made contact with Heath, who denied knowing Doreen.

After more thought, Heath decided to take the initiative. He telephoned Bournemouth Police Station and spoke with Detective Constable George Suter, explaining that he had dated a girl who was staying at the Royal Norfolk Hotel and he wanted to be quite sure that she was not the missing Doreen Marshall — although that was not the name by which she was known to him.

Suter thanked Group Captain Brooke for his public-spirited attitude and volunteered to send round a photograph of Doreen Marshall, but Heath said he would prefer to visit the police station. Bravado or suicide? Whichever, an appointment was made for 5.30 p.m. and Heath arrived with an officer's punctuality.

The first person Heath saw on entering the CID office at Bournemouth Police Station was himself, in the form of a wall-poster, which had been circulated by Scotland Yard. Suter was quick to spot the similarity and challenged Heath who vehemently denied it, although admitting a similarity.

Also in the CID department at the same time were the missing woman's father, Charles Marshall, and sister. Intoxicated with panache and self-esteem, Heath shook their hands warmly and proceeded to regale them with some fairly insensitive remarks about their loss.

Suter wasn't fooled, despite his humble rank. He told Group Captain Brooke that he would be detained for further questioning. Heath agreed, but made a pretext to return to his hotel to collect a jacket; Suter, however, arranged to have it collected.

There was only one jacket in the wardrobe of Room 81 at the Tollard Royal Hotel and this was searched by detectives, in the presence of Heath, at the police station. From the pockets they extracted the return half of a first-class London-Bournemouth rail ticket, one artificial pearl and a left-luggage receipt, dated June 23 and issued at Bournemouth West railway station.

The luggage Heath had deposited at the railway station was a battered suitcase, the contents of which included a leather, metal-tipped riding-whip and a scarf stained with blood and saliva. The detectives returned to Heath's hotel room to conduct a thorough search, and this time they came across a bloodstained handkerchief in a drawer. The handkerchief had been knotted tightly. Trapped in the knot were a number of dark human hairs.

Around 9.45 that same night, a Bournemouth detective informed Heath: 'There is no longer any doubt in our minds as to your indentity: you are Neville George Clevely Heath. Scotland Yard have been notified and Detective Chief Inspector Barratt is on his way and will be taking you back with him.' Heath agreed disgruntledly.

However, even before Barratt had arrived in Bournemouth, Heath was volunteering a statement, in which he wrote about his evening with Doreen Marshall:

'At about 11.30 p.m. the weather was clear and we left the hotel and sat on a seat near the hotel overlooking the sea. From this stage onwards my times are very vague because I had no wristwatch. We must have talked for at least an hour, probably longer, and then we walked down the slope towards the Pavilion. Miss Marshall did not wish me to accompany her but I insisted upon doing so — at least some of the way. I left her at the pier and watched her cross the road and enter the gardens. That was the last I saw of her.'

The search for Doreen Marshall ended on Monday, July 8. The previous evening, while walking her dog, Kathleen Evans, a waitress, came across a swarm of flies in a rhododendron bush along Branksome Dene Chine. During breakfast on the Monday, Miss Evans read in the newspapers about the police hunt for a body, possibly female, west of Bournemouth, in the area of the numerous chines — deep narrow ravines peculiar to Dorset and the Isle of Wight. She related to her parents her experience of the previous evening, emphasizing: 'I have an awful feeling. I *know* it's her. Please let me show you.'

Doreen Marshall had been stripped naked. The only item of

clothing remaining on her body was her left shoe. Her decorous black cocktail dress, matching bra and knickers, stockings and a smart yellow swagger coat had been tossed into a disorderly heap. Nearby, in a bush, were a compact and twenty-seven artificial pearls from a severed necklace.

The post-mortem examination revealed many injuries. The body was extensively bruised and cut. Ribs had been snapped causing a lung to be punctured and the cuts to her fingers were consistent with her having tried to defend herself against a knifeman's attack. The cause of death was haemorrhage of the carotid artery, but horrendous damage had also been inflicted while she was already dead. These after-death mutilations shocked even the most hardened policemen and experienced pathologists. Miss Marshall's vagina had been dismembered, a knife wound streaked from breast to breast, then plunging to her thigh, the right nipple had been bitten off and the left nipple was hanging by a single tissue thread. The body had been dragged over sand and something rough, like concrete, before being hidden, doubled-up, under a bush approximately ten yards from a path and a hundred yards from the beach.

Miss Marshall's handbag had not been among the rest of her clothes, but was found the next day, Tuesday, behind a beach chalet at Durley Chine, a couple of hundred yards from the body. Also missing were her wristwatch and a three-stone diamond ring, later to be recovered from a Bournemouth jeweller's shop, to which they had been sold after the murder by a man answering Heath's description.

It was also on the Tuesday that Barratt arranged for the receptionist at the Panama Club, and the taxi driver who had taken Margery Gardner and her escort to the Pembridge Court Hotel, to attend an identification parade at Scotland Yard. They both picked out Heath in the line-up. Barratt promptly charged Heath with the murder of Margery Gardner. When asked if he had anything to say, Heath said: 'No, not at the moment.'

The saliva-stained scarf, taken from the suitcase at Bournemouth West railway station, explained why no screams had been heard from Margery Gardner while she was being whipped and suffocated. Even without the gag, she might not have entreated Heath to spare her. During his investigation, Barratt discovered that Heath's first murder victim had been a masochist. Only a month before she went with Heath to the Pembridge Court Hotel, she was given a thrashing by him at another London hotel that might well have ended tragically had it not been for the timely intervention of a security officer. Mrs Gardner was prostrate on the bed with Heath, 'wild-eyed and crazy', looming over her with his whip, when an hotel detective used his master key to enter the room. Heath and Mrs Gardner were asked to leave *immediately*, and they departed holding hands.

On another occasion, also in a London hotel, shouts of 'Help!' and 'Murder!' sent guests running to a bedroom where Heath was beating another trussed-up young woman, who decided against prosecuting in order to avoid the inevitable scandalous publicity: she already had a husband, who knew nothing of her nocturnal adventures with Heath.

After Professor Simpson had examined Heath's whip, he told Barratt: 'It's an identical match. You have your man!'

Heath was also charged with the murder of Doreen Marshall, but was tried only for the Margery Gardner crime.

The trial began on September 24, 1946, in the Old Bailey's most famous Number One court. The judge was Mr Justice Morris. Heath, pleading 'Not Guilty', was defended by the redoubtable Joshua Casswell. Anthony Hawke, whose name aptly described his reputation, prosecuted. The trial lasted three days and was spectacular for its brevity.

The jury, of ten men and two women, retired at 4.35 p.m. on September 26. One hour later, they returned a unanimous 'guilty' verdict.

When asked by the judge if he had anything to say before the mandatory death sentence was passed, Heath replied 'Nothing'.

Pentonville Prison, in north London, was chosen as the place of execution. The date: October 16. The time: 9 a.m.

'Nine o'clock is a good time to die,' Heath said to his round-the-clock guards. 'There's plenty of time to have a good breakfast.'

At 7.30 on the morning of the execution, Heath tucked into a traditional English fry-up of two eggs, bacon, sausage, tomatoes and fried bread, followed by toast and marmalade and two mugs of tea.

Just before it was time for him to be led to the scaffold, Heath turned to the prison governor, who was standing next to the chaplain, and asked: 'Is it true that a condemned man is allowed one last wish?'

'That depends on the wish,' the governor replied cautiously.

'I'd love one last whisky,' said Heath.

The governor looked at his watch. Nothing could be allowed to delay the execution, but there was just time if he hurried.

As the governor scurried from the condemned cell, Heath called out: 'Make it a double!'

Neville George Clevely Heath was granted his last wish less than sixty seconds before the judicial noose broke his neck and he died the way he had enjoyed living, smelling of whisky.

One national newspaper journalist described Heath as 'probably the most dangerous criminal modern Britain has known'. It was his charm which made him so susceptible to women, and so lethal.

Branksome Dene Chine has changed very little since 1946. Holidaymakers in summer still use it as a short-cut to the West Beach. Locals walk their dogs along the snaking path. Birds nest in the prolific vegetation. On sunny days, families picnic on the slopes. Lovers enjoy the sound of the sea at dusk. Pine trees stand stiff as sentinels: sinister secrets of the past are safe with them.

Under the bush where the flies found the hapless Doreen Marshall is a bed of yellow and blue flowers. They cannot be seen anywhere else in the chine, and bloom every summer as an eternal wreath. They are forget-me-nots.

2

□□■□□

Whitechapel, London, E1

■ THE creaking metal pub signboard, depicting a man shrouded in a black Victorian cloak and stalking with sinister intent an ill-lit, narrow cobbled street, told the one-hundred-year-old story.

A wind, as sharp as the wicked knife that made this unholy patch of the East End so infamous, cut across the corner where Commercial Street allowed Fournier Street to push in.

A small group of women protesters, bearing banners with melancholy messages, ambulated unhappily on a piece of pavement steeped in criminal history. Marie Jeanette Kelly had monopolized the same street corner on the night of November 9, 1888. I followed in those confident steps to the unpretentious pub, which until 1974, was *The Ten Bells*. Now it is called *Jack the Ripper*. As far as the world of murder is concerned, this has to be the prime location.

Miss Kelly, a twenty-four-year-old prostitute, had gone to *The Ten Bells* looking for business. It was her 'local', and on the last night of her life it had, as usual, been crowded.

Tony Wright, on the upright, honky piano, tried his best to liven up proceedings with a medley of vaudeville tunes but even his efforts were not enough. 'No fear of anyone in 'ere gettin' done-in tonight; they're already dead!,' quipped the cockney pianist, reaching on top of the piano for the beer that had been bought for him by one of the pub's few regulars. Earlier, he'd made another droll observation during an impromptu history lesson on nineteenth-century crime:

'Bloody sight more people were killed by the Duke of Wellington than the Ripper!'

The women outside — social workers, artists, market workers, councillors and teachers — would not have been amused. They were protesting against a pub 'celebrating murder; the very brutal murder of women'. One banner blazened the message, 'Ten Bells Rings Better'. It was the name of the pub that angered them. 'Would anyone dream of opening a "Yorkshire Ripper" pub in Leeds?' one of them asked. 'Or a Michael Ryan pub in rural Hungerford?'

Meanwhile, the landlord's wife, Yvonne Ostrowski, was mixing me, in exchange for 90p, a blood-red Ripper Tipple. Mysteriously, she was unforthcoming as to the ingredients.

Also on offer were 'Ripper' T-shirts. 'How disgusting!' complained a young woman, who had given up her job to become a professional campaigner for women's causes. I felt that she had a point.

On the high walls were copies of the *Illustrated Police Gazette* of the autumn of 1888, reporting the hunt for the monster who had introduced mutilation and disembowelment to the slum streets of Victorian Whitechapel. There were also photographs of the claustrophobic courtyards and labyrinthine alleys where the six 'Jack the Ripper' victims had perished, plus a portrait of a Victorian woman. 'Ripper' buffs, mainly American tourists, were continually asking publican Erni Ostrowski, or his wife, which of the victims was the lady on the wall — Martha Turner, Mary Ann Nichols, Annie Chapman, Elizabeth Stride, Catherine Eddowes or Marie Jeanette Kelly. The answer always came as a disappointment. 'She's none of them — just my great-great-grandmother who's reputed to have been an alcoholic, so I felt that the wall of the pub was the most suitable place for her', revealed Mrs Ostrowski.

The Ten Bells wouldn't have been very different in 1888: it had always been a bit of a spit-and-sawdust establishment, appropriate for its milieu, and it had not aged gracefully. Since my visit, it has been tarted-up thus loosing much of its raw, pristine character.

I closed my eyes and amid the clinking cacophony of bar sounds, allowed my imagination to take me back to that roistering night when Marie Jeanette Kelly left *The Ten Bells*, disgusted at the lack of interest among the male tipplers. I departed through the same door and loitered on the drab, windswept corner, just as she would have done. The protesters had dispersed, but a policeman, taking no chances had lingered across the road, just in case fun should deteriorate into fighting.

I checked my bearings. Directly opposite was Spitalfields Market, eerily silent at that time of night. Out of view, but only a couple of turns from Spitalfields, was Petticoat Lane, the venue of London's most famous Sunday morning street market, though a ghost town after dark, especially during the week. My route was due south, towards the slow-beating heart of Whitechapel, the Tower and the Pool of London. The furtive moon appeared hooded and the rain in the air was more of a threat than a promise. The clouds, spurred by a westerly wind, were responsible for an optical illusion of stampeding stars.

The network of infested alleys, lanes and courtyards of 1888 have gone, but the soulessness and scruffiness still pervade. The gin-palaces, doss-houses and brothels have been replaced by warehouses, boarded-up shops and inner-city dereliction. The gas lamps were retired years ago, but electricity has served only to lengthen the shadows and illuminate the darkness. Few people live there any more. Everyone had moved out, or was in the process of moving. Rot was rampant.

On the corner of Fashion Street — such a sick misnomer! — a middle-aged whore approached me. Marie Kelly might well have picked up her last customer within a few yards of the same place, but she would have been dressed rather more modestly than her sisters of the 1980s: an ankle-length dress instead of a mini-skirt, bootees rather than high-heeled stiletto shoes, and possibly a bonnet tilted on her head and shawl drawn around her shoulders. Crossing the busy main road, she would have been dodging horse-drawn carriages, not cars.

Miss Kelly, the youngest and last of the 'Ripper's' victims, rented a room in Miller's Court, off Dorset Street, which was later re-named Duval Street, though it is not marked on any map of London. Today, Duval Street links Commercial Street and Crispin Street, though its name does not appear. It does not even have a postal address: it is a road no one wishes to recognize.

The cesspit of a house in which Miss Kelly lived was on a site that is now a multi-storey car park, just north of White's Row, where her screams were heard at 3.30 in the morning of her murder. In fact, all of her neighbours heard her cries, but no one went to her aid. When asked by the police why not, the unanimous explanation was that screams of 'Murder!' were a common occurrence from Miss Kelly's squalid abode. Being attacked was — and still is — one of the professional hazards of prostitution. Most of her clients were loud-mouthed, uncouth villains. Those who could afford more went west, not east.

At 10.45 a.m. on November 9, 1888, the rent-collector thumped on Miss Kelly's door. When there was no reply, he pounded with his fist, yelling: 'I know you're in there. Open up, you slut, or I'll bust in. You owe money and I'm not shiftin' till I've got what's due, so 'elp me — and you!'

The grubby window beside the front door at street level was broken, giving the rent-collector a clear view of the dirty and unkempt interior. Miss Kelly occupied one room, the size of which today would be too small even to be classified a 'modest bed-sit'. The rent-collector thought he could see someone on the bed, but the place was in such disarray that he wasn't sure. It was understandable that he supposed Miss Kelly was still recovering from the night before, as usual. The state of the room indicated that she had been brawling with one of her drunken clients; probably over money. But as the caller peered through the gloom, he must have begun to feel uneasy. For a start, Miss Kelly's head did not appear to be attached to her body. Such a phenomenon was unknown to him during the sober hours! It had to be a mirage, but there was no mistaking the blood on the walls, floor and bedding. There was only one way to establish the truth.

The rent-collector was surprised to find the door unlocked.

He hadn't thought of trying it before because Miss Kelly, however confused she might have been after a day on the streets, always bolted herself in before collapsing for the night. Now he was alarmed.

Placed in the centre of the pillow, almost ceremoniously, like a crown jewel on a display cushion, was a human heart. In the manner of Christmas-decoration streamers, Miss Kelly's entrails had been looped around the room, also framing a picture on the wall. Her head had indeed been cut almost completely from her neck. One can only imagine the horror experienced by such a grisly discovery.

The whistle-blowing police arrived by foot and carriage. One look was enough to substantiate their worst fear — 'Jack the Ripper' had struck again.

In an open grate, they found the ashes of an assortment of rags, which, they surmised, had been burned by the 'Ripper' in order to provide sufficient light with which to perform his gruesome surgery.

The police were satisfied that the terrifying screams at 3.30 a.m. substantiated the time of death. Missing, though, were witnesses who could help them trace Miss Kelly's movements between leaving *The Ten Bells* pub and three hours later when she was butchered in her humble lodgings.

One street girl told the police: 'She would have been walking, looking for men. Walking round and round, up and down, standing on corners, under lamps, at the entrance to alleys, winking, smiling, beckoning. She'd take men back to her room, they would fight over money and if she was lucky, she'd be paid something. Then she'd go back to her patch. No man will ever own up to being with her: more than he dare do.'

The police reasoned that 'Jack the Ripper', whoever he was, could easily have followed Miss Kelly back to her place as she escorted a customer. He could have lurked in the shadows, waiting for the man to leave, and then entered Miss Kelly's room before she returned to the street. Conversely, he might have allowed himself to be propositioned in an alley, which would have been more consistent with the previous murders. However, police were just guessing, and were no nearer solving the mystery of the identity of 'Jack the Ripper' than they were when the killing spree had begun on August 7.

Later, at the inquest, it was reported that no body organs had been taken away. This had been a chilling feature of some of the previous cases.

Students of the 'Jack the Ripper' legend, which is what it has become, still argue about the number of victims, but six, beginning with Martha Turner, seems to be the general consensus. Turner (there is uncertainty regarding the spelling: it could have been Tabram) was touting for business on the August Bank Holiday Monday, when she accosted a soldier, who was already 'the worse for drink'. Instead of going straight to her miserable little dwelling in George Yard, now Gunthorpe Street, a dank, unlit alley intersecting Whitechapel High Street, Turner agreed to go drinking in a nearby pub, *The Angel and Crown*, with the soldier.

Martha Turner's body was found at five o'clock the following morning on a first-floor landing in George Yard Buildings, a tatty tenement block. The pathologist counted thirty-nine stab wounds. He was also able to establish, beyond all doubt, that two weapons had been used on Turner and that the killer was ambidextrous. The medical evidence went further: one of the weapons was a knife with a very long blade and could even have been a bayonet. However, some of the wounds had been caused by a surgeon's scalpel.

Not unnaturally, the police suspected that the killer, initially dubbed 'The Whitechapel Murderer', could be a soldier or doctor, and possibly a combination of the two, such as a military surgeon. They soon located one of Turner's few friends, another prostitute, whose street name was Pearly Poll. She told the police that she had been with Turner the previous night, drinking with soldiers in *The Angel and Crown* and had left the pub in a foursome, all of them 'well an' truly pickled pink!' It was midnight as they tottered the few hundred yards to the arched entrance of George Yard, where the couples parted, Pearly leading her client to her place and Turner, presumably, taking the other soldier to George Yard Buildings.

The investigating officers were excited by the introduction into the case of soldiers, bearing in mind the medical report which mentioned the possibility of a bayonet having been used. A large contingent of soldiers, fitting the description of those drinking in *The Angel and Crown* during the holiday weekend, were known to be stationed at the Tower of London, and that is where the police concentrated their early inquiries. The garrison commander agreed to arrange a full parade of every man on his establishment — including officers — for what must have been the most bizarre inspection in British Army history. The men were lined up, and after the roll call proved that no one was missing, Pearly Poll was led along the ranks, stopping to look into the face of each soldier. Two hours later, Pearly had failed to recognize either the soldier who paid for sex with her, or the one who had gone with Turner. Later, she was to tell another whore that she reckoned half the regiment at the Tower had 'been with' her, but not on the night in question.

The police were not convinced by Pearly's testimony and believed that she knew more than she was divulging. However, they could not induce her to remember more. Every uniform at the Tower was examined, but bloodstains were found neither on these, nor on the bayonets, all of which were accounted for. Neither did the police have any more luck with their search among the brick-and-timber shanty-town environment for the murder weapons.

Mary Ann Nichols, an alcoholic prostitute, had been a resident of a doss-house in Thrawl Street, paying fourpence a night for her wooden bed without mattress but she had been evicted because she was penniless. Nichols was married but her husband, a printer's machinist, had disowned her seven years previously. Although she was forty-two years old, Mrs Nichols, known with little affection on the streets as Polly, looked positively geriatric. She was last seen alive at 2.30 a.m.

on Friday, August 31, when she was parading under a gas lamp on the corner of Osborn Street, complaining to another prostitute about the lack of business. Three-quarters-of-an-hour later she was dead, and a cartwright stumbled over her body at the entrance to the Old Stable Yard directly opposite Essex Wharf, at the west end of Bucks Row (now Durward Street) which backed on to the London Hospital. This strengthened the connection between the 'Ripper' and the medical profession.

Her body was taken to the mortuary at the Old Montague Street Workhouse, where an autopsy proved that she had been disemboweled after having had her throat cut and two front teeth extracted. A bruise on her mouth was evidence that a hand had been used to mute her screams while the death-stroke was delivered. No one in the congested neighbourhood had heard a sound.

Another evicted prostitute, Annie Chapman, became the next victim. She had been living in a lodging-house in Dorset Street and on the night of September 8, she is believed to have met the 'Ripper' outside No. 29, Hanbury Street — a home for sixteen people. It is highly likely that she made the first approach, in view of her occupation. Together, they went along a passageway beside the house until they came to the rear yard, where Chapman, who was forty-seven years old, was found at 6 a.m. Her kidneys and ovaries had been taken, and, as in the Nichols case, her two front teeth were missing. She had also almost been decapitated — a feature of the first murder — although this time the head had been tied back with a handkerchief. Around her feet had been sprinkled some copper coins, in a shape that seemed to represent a symbol or secret sign, hence the reference to Freemasons in a number of works on the mystery.

Under a tap in the yard, the police came across part of an envelope embossed with the crest of the Sussex Regiment. Beside the bloodstained envelope was a leather apron. Despite so many people sleeping nearby, again no one was woken.

The police did make an arrest this time in the form of Pizer, a Polish Jew cobbler, nicknamed 'Leather Apron', but there was no incriminating evidence against him, only malicious gossip among an understandably terrified community. Under pressure from the panicking public, the police were desperate for a breakthrough, but the extent of the case against Mr Pizer was that he wore an apron at work! Accordingly, he was released without ever being charged.

At one time, this whole area of London had been a resplendent mix of architectural elegance and overt wealth. The halcyon days for Whitechapel and Spitalfields came during the 1700s, brought about by an influx of refugee Huguenot silk-weavers. However, the silk-weaving bonanza was short-lived and by the time 'Jack the Ripper' was terrorizing the East End, the big houses had disintegrated into multiple dwellings, with ten to twenty people, in some cases, occupying a single room. Newer, though no more salubrious, were the brick huts, which were also overcrowded. Disease and destitution were rife in epidemic proportions. Considering this context, the 'Ripper' was the least of women's worries. The slums no longer exist, but a hundred years have done nothing to dispel the atmosphere of depression.

A threat of more murders to come was presaged on September 28 in a letter to the Central News Agency. Signing himself *'Jack the Ripper'*, the writer warned: 'I am down on whores and shant quit ripping them till I do get buckled'. This letter was reproduced in the Sunday newspapers and the self-attributed appellation, 'Jack the Ripper', instantly installed The Whitechapel Murderer as the worst of his kind.

Unfortunately, the 'Ripper' proved to be a man of his word. At 1 a.m. on September 30, Louis Deimschutz, a street-hawker and secretary of a Jewish working men's club, steered his horse and cart into Berner Street (now Henriques Street). His destination was the International Workers Educational Club, about halfway down Berner Street — later to become the location of a school. As he dismounted in the Club's backyard, he stepped on a woman's body — that of Elizabeth Stride, Swedish by birth, and nicknamed 'Long Liz' because she was so tall. Her throat had been slit, but she was still warm, fuelling speculation that the 'Ripper' had been disturbed by the inconvenient and unexpected arrival of Deimschutz. Another witness saw a 'youngish man, carrying a black bag, hurrying from Berner Street' at the approximate time of the murder.

As uniformed officers were converging on Berner Street, Catherine Eddowes, a prostitute who was forever in and out of jail, was being bailed from Bishopsgate Police Station, having been arrested for drunken behaviour and brawling. A Constable Watkins, on his usual beat, walked along Church Passage, today St James' Passage — an echoing alley joining Mitre Square and Duke Street. He was oscillating his flashlight, on the lookout for the usual drunks who littered the floors of such places, but not so that night. Fifteen minutes later, PC Watkins returned to Mitre Square, which was no longer deserted. At the entrance to Church Passage, surrounded by dusty offices and rancid warehouses, was the body of forty-three-year-old Catherine Eddowes, her face mutilated, her stomach ripped and her left kidney and intestines cut out and pillaged.

An intensive search of the area yielded a useful clue: a portion of Eddowes's apron, bearing bloodstains, outside the Wentworth Model Dwellings in Goulston Street, a parallel road to Petticoat Lane. This proved that the 'Ripper' had doubled back, consistent with his heading for the London Hospital, further strengthening the theory that, by profession, he was at the very least *connected* with medicine. Certainly a knowledge of anatomy and some experience of pathology would have been mandatory for such swift dissection.

A second letter, written in red ink and once again signed *'Jack the Ripper'*, had been posted to the Central News Agency just a couple of hours following the double murder. It contained an apology for not having sent the 'ears' to the police: the post-mortem report on Catherine Eddowes referred to an apparent attempt to amputate her ears. Perhaps he had been disturbed during the second murder that night as well as the first? In fact, it is more probable than possible. 'Jack' could have watched covertly from a doorway as PC Watkins patrolled his beat. He wouldn't have expected the constable to return so quickly to Mitre Square. In his red-ink second letter, 'Jack' also made the point that Elizabeth Stride 'squealed a bit'.

Sir Charles Warren had been the Metropolitan Police Commissioner for two years, but he, too, was destined to become a victim of 'Jack the Ripper'. Desperate for results, he planted undercover policemen and decoys on the streets of Whitechapel, and he also sanctioned the involvement of vigilante groups, but to no avail. 'Jack' was never caught, and the beleaguered police commissioner was compelled to resign, his career cut off in its prime.

We shall never know for sure the identity of the man who was forever to give Whitechapel a bad name. We *do* know that millions of people all over the world, through several generations, have been mesmerized by the puzzle. However, most of the books written on the subject should be banished to the fiction shelves. If the professionals could not unravel the mystery in 1888, there is no chance of a denouement a century later from the amateur sleuths: that is the only certainty in this case.

In this game of speculation, I should have to put my money on George Chapman, the favourite candidate of Chief Inspector Abberline, who was in charge of the investigations.

Chapman's real name was Severin Antoniovitch Klosovski. He was born on December 14, 1865, in Nargornak, Poland. When he was fifteen years old, he had become an apprentice surgeon in Zvolen, but he failed his medical examinations and never qualified as a doctor. After six years of apprenticeship, he left Zvolen to become a barber, also performing minor operations, which was not uncommon in those times. Even in England, people went to their barber for small operations, which explains the origin of the blood-red and white poles outside barbers' shops.

After marrying, Chapman joined the Russian Army, but within eighteen months he was sailing for London, settling in Whitechapel and taking a job as a barber in the High Street. By the August of 1888, he had set up a small barber's business in the basement of George Yard Buildings, where Martha Turner was murdered during the Bank Holiday.

Chapman committed bigamy, marrying Lucy Baderski who was also Polish, only a few months later to be joined by his legal wife who decided to leave Poland. In a bizarre domestic triangle, the three of them lived together in the same house, until Chapman and his illegal wife emigrated, in 1890, to America.

Chapman could not resist other women and within a year of going to America, Lucy had returned. The following year, 1892, Chapman was also back in London and a trial reconciliation was a failure, leading to a permanent separation. By this time, they had two children, who went with their mother.

His next live-in lover was an Annie Chapman, bearing the same name as one of 'Jack the Ripper's victims. It was around the time Annie Chapman walked out on him that he changed his name to George Chapman, never again to be known as Klosovski.

The next woman in his life was a Mary Spinks, a heavy drinker who was separated from her husband. After a brief affair, she moved in with Chapman and they bought property in Hastings, Sussex, where they were known as Mr and Mrs Chapman, although they never married. Mrs Spinks had private means and she invested in a barber's shop for her lover. While Chapman clipped hair and shaved chins, Mary played a piano in a corner of the shop. This proved a profitable gimmick.

Chapman, however, was never satisfied and was always hankering after London's night life. Accordingly, to placate his vagaries, they bought a pub called *The Prince of Wales* in Bartholomew Square, off City Road, London, where Mary died on Christmas Day, 1897, a doctor certifying that tuberculosis was the cause of death.

Chapman went through another bigamous marriage, this time with his barmaid, Bessie Taylor, a farmer's daughter. They moved pub several times, until Bessie died on February 13, 1901, of 'exhaustion from vomiting and diarrhoea'.

Bessie's place in Chapman's bed was taken by Maud Marsh, another barmaid, who came from Croydon. He was now running *The Crown* pub in Union Street, the Borough. Soon Maud was suffering from similar symptoms to those which had afflicted Bessie. Maud's mother, fearing for her daughter's health, went with her own GP, a Dr Grapel, to Chapman's pub. After examining Maud, Dr Grapel diagnosed arsenic poisoning. Maud died on October 22, 1902. Chapman's GP, a Dr Stoker, received a note from Dr Grapel and declined to issue a death certificate. An autopsy proved that indeed Maud had been poisoned — not with arsenic, but antimony.

Chapman was duly charged on October 25, Edward VII's coronation procession day, with the murder of Maud. Chief Inspector Abberline was to exclaim: 'At last the Ripper has been caught!'

Chapman was hanged on April 7, 1903.

But was he *really* the 'Ripper'?

Chapman is a better candidate than most. He had a shop in the square where one of the 'Ripper' victims was slain. Every night during that period from August to November, 1888, he was known to stalk the streets of Whitechapel and Spitalfields looking for women. He answered the description of a man seen hurrying from the vicinity of two of the bodies. Most importantly, he had been a surgeon's apprentice for six years and had performed minor surgery ever since, possessing all the necessary tools. Finally, his life had come to an end on the gallows for the murder of a woman.

The 'Jack the Ripper' buffs who dismiss Chapman's claims to the highest office of infamy do so on the suspect grounds that knifemen do not become poisoners. I believe they have missed the point. 'Jack the Ripper' was not a knifeman by conventional standards. He was a clinical dissector. Undoubtedly, Chapman was a bitter man, feeling cheated because he had been denied a medical degree. Murdering whores, whom he may well have regarded as subhuman, could have been his own insane way of retaliation. It is no use applying logic to the mind of a madman, although that does not mean that 'Jack the Ripper' was without intelligence. Quite the opposite. Insanity and intelligence often go in tandem. When Chapman disposed of his 'wives', there was orthodox motive in his madness, hence the means that would give him a sporting chance of eschewing detection. If he had knifed the women with whom he had an overt emotional attachment, he would have been the one and only suspect from the outset, also drawing attention once again to his credentials for being the 'Ripper'. He had been near the top of the list of suspects during the original inquiries into the 'Jack the Ripper' killings. Chapman murdered with guile, when it was necessary — and so did the 'Ripper', in his own extrovert way.

For many years there have been rumours that the area around the old site of No. 29, Hanbury Street, where Annie Chapman died, is haunted. Numerous people, including two extremely level-headed policemen, have been privy to 'very odd' experiences within a few yards of the exact spot where Annie was mutilated. Both, on separate occasions, were patrolling this particular patch late at night when they heard deep breathing and the sound of a scuffle, followed by a woman's stifled scream. The noise of the struggle continued unabated until they were 'at the centre' of the phenomenon, yet there was nothing whatsoever to see. Reports of similar occurrences are well-documented, and there are many people who believe that there is a genuine psychic phenomenon related to the 'Ripper' killings and many other similar cases. Peter Underwood, in his book *Jack the Ripper, One Hundred Years of Mystery*, writes: 'There is a theory that under certain conditions and in certain circumstances tragic and violent happenings leave behind an impression on the atmosphere, a kind of atmospheric photograph.' He argues that, given the right conditions, these 'impressions' can reappear to be seen or heard by anyone present at that moment. It would certainly explain so many of the apparently inexplicable encounters chronicled by countless people at the locations of harrowing incidents, not merely the scenes of murders.

If only the ghost of 'Jack the Ripper' could step forward to be recognized, although, on reflection, perhaps that is not such a good idea. To resolve the mystery as to the identity of the murderer would be to put an end to all the speculation, and to the many fascinating and ingenious theories surrounding these gruesome murders.

3

□□■□□

No. 16, Wardle Brook Avenue

■ THEY had come from near and far like ghouls to a public execution, their faces as bleak as the backdrop of black peat moorland. This was not a happy occasion. Happiness had deserted Wardle Brook Avenue, Hattersley, twenty-two years ago, with the screams and supplications of the tortured innocent. These had remained ever since, like a vindictive poltergeist, to haunt this quiet road of neat council houses in the eerie shadows of those mist-shrouded moors, which, through the ages, have contained so many ghastly secrets.

Although the women wore funereal black, the mourning has been incessant since the bodies of Lesley Ann Downey and John Kilbride were dug out of their pitiful makeshift graves on unhallowed moorland all those years ago. Since then, the skeletal remains of Pauline Reade have also been rescued from the desolate netherworld of Saddleworth Moor, now a part of Greater Manchester, as is the small community of Hattersley, regarded by most people as a part of Hyde. Keith Bennett also has an unhallowed grave somewhere on that godforsaken moorland: Hindley and Brady cannot remember where they buried him and sinister Saddleworth, a conspiratorial presence, provides no clues.

This was an unconventional funeral. The pallbearers were council workmen, wearing bright yellow helmets. The hearse was a bulldozer and the coffin to be ignominiously buried was No. 16, Wardle Brook Avenue, where child killers Myra Hindley and Ian Brady had lived together, and murdered together, sharing their lust for sadism and all things inspired by the devil. Within those flimsy walls Brady had axed and strangled Edward Evans, while Hindley watched.

But memories cannot be bulldozed away. Even though this house of horrors has finally been razed, everything it represents still lives on to haunt and torment. Forever, this desecrated plot of land will remain the devil's own. No amount of demolition or rebuilding will serve either to console, or to expunge the bloody stains on a nation's conscience. Something inside the nation died at No. 16, Wardle Brook Avenue — such an ordinary address for such appalling infamy!

A spontaneous round of applause accompanied the first blow to the home of craven child predators Hindley and Brady, both of whom are still serving life sentences today. 'I've waited so long for this day,' said one neighbour. 'It's very little in terms of revenge when you consider what they did, but it's the first time we've witnessed anything tangible against them. As their house tumbles, I feel that the lifeblood is being knocked out of them. It's not, of course. How I wish it were! But there is some satisfaction from it. I wouldn't call this an execution, but more an exorcism. We have lived with too many ghosts for too long.'

Another woman, who had lived in the Avenue for more than twenty-five years, said: 'Now perhaps we'll have some peace. Ever since the trial, all that time ago, we've been plagued by sightseers — sometimes as many as ten or twelve coach loads a day from as far afield as Scotland and the south coast — taking photographs, stealing anything, even blades of grass, and stomping all over gardens. We were sick of it.'

Still the sightseers come, even when there is nothing to see. Forever No. 16, Wardle Brook Avenue will be the antithesis of the shrine; a monument, rather, to the depths of depravity to which human beings can descend.

Even Brady himself purported to be offended by the tasteless behaviour of tourists on the day of demolition! In a letter to his long-standing pen-friend, Mrs Moya Minns, an office worker at an engineering firm in Slough, Berkshire, he wrote:

'I suppose you heard of the grotesque scenes which occurred when our house was demolished because people wouldn't live in it as previous occupiers said they heard ghostly screams. Anyway, crowds descended on the house as it was a last chance to grab 'macabre souvenirs'. A neighbour counted fifty or sixty cars at one time and others came in the dead of night.'

One of the demolition workmen almost fainted as the house came down. 'It was a cold day, as you know,' he explained, 'but suddenly my whole body became very clammy. My neck felt tight, as if I was being choked, and I was desperate for air, even though I was outdoors the whole time. Then the ground seemed to be giving way beneath my feet and my head became filled with human howling, a 'wailing at the wall' kind of ear-bashing, and I had to clasp my hands to the side of my face. It sounds daft when I talk about it now, but at the time it was scary, like something from a horror movie. I had the feeling that we were knocking down a catacomb and releasing some very angry, avenging souls. I never want to go back. I do believe the evil lives on. There were demons in my head that day.'

Number 16, Wardle Brook Avenue had looked no different from all the other post-war, red-brick houses in the same road. It was an end-of-terrace property with white, ranch-style fencing and an overgrown bush in the front garden. But there the similarity ended. Ever since the arrest of Hindley and Brady, a succession of occupants have been driven out by cries they have alleged to be those of tortured children.

The last tenants were Brian and Margaret Dunne and their three children. From the moment they moved in, they complained of dampness that ran in rivulets down the walls, sometimes turning reddish in colour, especially where the children slept. Although all the houses had been built at the same time, No. 16 was the only one to have a problem with damp.

'It wasn't ordinary dampness, the walls were crying and bleeding,' Mr Dunne insisted. 'The walls were smeared with the tears of dead children. The house was cursed, and can you wonder?'

The families who have set their roots in Wardle Brook Avenue are not wealthy folk. All of them come from a north-west working-class background, of which they are fiercely proud. They have a strong sense of morality but like to enjoy life. They are exceptionally tolerant and without malice, but their faces are grim at the prospect of parole for Hindley. 'If she does ever get out, whatever the pretext, she'll be killed within hours of her release,' one female Hattersley resident pledged. 'Relatives of the children who were buried on the moors have sworn to kill Hindley if she's ever freed, but that wouldn't be fair on them. They would be quickly arrested and jailed, and no one wants that, especially the police. Contingency plans have been drawn up; names will go into a hat, men and women — me included. The draw will be made in the *New Inn* Pub and the lucky winner will do the business. For me, it would be both an honour and a pleasure. The others would then provide me with an alibi. It's been thought out very carefully, believe me. To be absolutely honest, I don't think the police would work up much sweat looking for Hindley's killer. If they did, I'm sure the taxpayers would have something to say about the waste of public money.'

I'll never forget my first visit to No. 16, Wardle Brook Avenue, long after the murder there. The living room was squarish and compact with just enough space for a divan-bed, table, a couple of chairs and a portable television. How could a man have had room to wield an axe? Yet in that very limited space, Brady had hacked away at seventeen-year-old Edward Evans, who had been chosen at random for elimination. At Brady's side, urging him on, had been Myra Hindley, the high priestess of perversion and a devout disciple of the Marquis de Sade. Somehow Evans had survived the axe assault, only to have a cushion cover thrust over his head and an electric flex tightened around his neck.

Hindley's brother-in-law, David Smith, had also been in that chamber of horrors as a reluctant onlooker, lured there by his sister-in-law under false pretences in a lurid attempt to corrupt him. Blood had been everywhere, even on the pink walls and white emulsioned ceiling. Hindley had gone in search of a bucket of water, a mop and some rags, while Brady smoked a cigarette and drank German white wine. Upstairs, sleeping through this appalling murder was Hindley's feeble grandmother, Ellen Maybury, who was almost bedridden.

In the bedroom next to where Granny Maybury was sleeping in peace and blissful ignorance, was a similar-sized modest room, containing an old table and chair, one single bed and a wardrobe. This was Hindley's bedroom, but she seldom slept there, preferring to snuggle beside her sadistic lover in the divan-bed downstairs.

After the walls, linoleum, ceiling, carpets and furniture had been scrubbed spotlessly clean that fateful night of Wednesday, October 6, 1965, Hindley had returned to the kitchen for polythene sheets where she was fussed over by two dogs, her mongrel pet, Puppet, and her grandmother's Lassie. However, there were far more pressing matters making demands on her, such as helping to truss up their victim, pushing his knees under his chin, binding his hands behind his back and fixing a noose around his neck. 'Eddie's a dead weight!' Brady had mocked as he and his accomplice had carried the body upstairs, finally squeezing it under the bed in Myra's room.

As I went up that same narrow staircase to the unpretentious landing, I tried to visualize Hindley and Brady struggling with the corpse. It must have been a considerable task. The first bedroom had been Mrs Maybury's, where she had woken up with a start as the killers dropped the body as they passed. Out of breath, Hindley had gone coolly into the old woman's room to tell the lie: 'It was only me, Gran. I dropped the tape-recorder on my toe.'

With two more paces I was on the threshold of the bedroom where Evans had been left. As the door creaked open an inch or two at a time, I let my imagination take me back to 8.30 a.m. on October 7, 1965, when Superintendent Robert Talbot had stood on the same exposed floorboard, having been directed to the house by David Smith. To avoid alerting Brady and

Hindley, he had disguised himself as a bread-delivery man, carrying a basket of freshly-baked loaves. Inside the bedroom, Talbot had seen a human foot protruding from under the bed.

I shuddered as I peered under another similarly-positioned bed. Brian and Margaret Dunne had, on several occasions, seen the apparition of a young man on that bed. They were not the only people to report the sightings of a ghost in that room. It was always a youth lying face up on the bed. 'It was never aggressive, never threatening,' said one former tenant. 'Usually it appeared late at night, but not always. I can't recall it ever moving. It would lie on the bed and immediately water would stream down the walls. It's not easy to live with a ghost, even a harmless one. I didn't mind too much, but the kids were terrified. The dampness was bad for our health. The kids were never without a cold and my wife began to suffer from rheumatism. In the end, we just had to get out.'

Once again I was reminded of the electrical impulse wave theory as an explanation for ghosts; the implantation of a telepathic image from a brain under stress, for example, during a murder, which could last for years. However, if the ghost *was* that of Edward Evans, why did it not appear in the living room, where he was murdered so violently and all the stress was suffered? Maybe they were seeing the ghost of Lesley Ann Downey who endured hell upstairs. However, most witnesses of the apparition have described a young man. There is no answer, merely speculations and questions. But still, even after the house has gone, people talk of a 'silver, ghostly silhouette' that 'floats' across the site where No. 16, Wardle Brook Avenue once stood. These are neither unstable, irrational people, nor drunks or over-imaginative romancers; one is a policeman and another has been employed in the council housing department for more than twenty years.

Certainly the policeman has been trained to observe and report facts lucidly, without either emotion or embellishment. On two successive nights he saw, 'beyond all doubt', the 'translucent outline of a youth' leave the pavement and disappear, 'evaporating like a puff of smoke, whitish and flaky', where No. 16 had been. On both occasions, the policeman was sitting behind the wheel of his stationary car and questioned whether he might have been mistaken. 'That's something I've asked myself over and over again. The answer has to be an unequivocal *no*. I'm not saying I saw a ghost. I'm not saying it was Edward Evans. That's for others to evaluate. I can only tell you what I saw. It was human in shape, but had no substance to it. As I said, it sort of floated, then vanished. I got out of my car and went in pursuit, both times, but there was nothing; not a sound. If it had been anybody, I would have heard movement; running feet or the slamming of a door. I don't like talking about it really. Policemen aren't supposed to believe in ghosts, are they? If my mates knew, they'd think I was going off my rocker. The strange thing is that I've always laughed at people who believe in the supernatural. Now I'm not so sure. I'm no longer the sceptic that I was.'

For me, the living room at No. 16, Wardle Brook Avenue had been alive with violent imagery. After the murder of Evans, the cleaning up and removal of the body, Hindley had brought in a pot of tea. Just minutes after such calculated human slaughter, she had been sitting drinking tea and rejoicing in the butchery. 'You should have seen the look on his face,' she had said to Brady. 'The blow registered in his eyes.'

No wonder no one could live in a place with such macabre memories. For two years before demolition, it was used as a daytime office by the workmen who were installing central heating on the council estate, of which Wardle Brook Avenue is a part.

The other victims of Hindley and Brady died no less horrendously, though little is known about the circumstances of the death of sixteen-year-old Pauline Reade, who disappeared on the night of July 12, 1963, on her way from her home in Wiles Street, Gorton (a grim suburb of Manchester) to a dance at the Railway Social Club.

At the time of Pauline's abduction, Hindley and Brady were

living together in a Victorian 'two-up two-down' at 7 Bannock Street, Gorton — also the home of Mrs Maybury.

Their next victim had been schoolboy John Kilbride, aged twelve, who often worked on Saturdays at the street market in Ashton-under-Lyne, his home town, some six miles from Manchester's city centre. On Saturday, November 23, 1963, the day after President Kennedy was assassinated, John Kilbride went with his friend, John Ryan, also twelve years old, to see the film *The Mongols* at a local cinema. By five o'clock they were among the stalls of the Ashton-under-Lyne market, doing a couple of odd jobs for a trader who was selling carpets. Very shortly afterwards John Ryan met a couple of old friends. By then, it was already dark and he decided to head for home with the other boys, leaving John Kilbride on his own. John was to remain missing for almost two years, only to be found among the rocks of Saddleworth Moor.

Ten-year-old Lesley Ann Downey was tortured to death by Hindley and Brady on Boxing Day, 1964, after being subjected to all kinds of obscenities and sexual abuse, including being photographed naked. Those atrocities were tape-recorded by the killers, providing damning evidence against them at their trial, which began at Chester Assizes on April 19, 1966, before an all-male jury. Other incriminating exhibits were photographs of Hindley and Brady gloating over the children's graves on the moors. The trial lasted fourteen days and took the jury just two hours and sixteen minutes to reach a verdict.

What were the backgrounds of these two murderers?

Myra Hindley was a 'war baby', born on July 23, 1942. Her father, Robert Hindley, was in the Parachute Regiment. Her mother, Nellie, had two girls to look after single-handedly, Myra being the elder. At four years old, she went to live with her grandmother at No. 7, Bannock Street. By the time Hindley was attending Ryder Brow Secondary School, she was already regarded by teachers and contemporaries as a loner. She was not a particularly attractive child, with her short brown army-style hair, and certainly qualified for the playground taunts of 'Plain Jane' from the boys. The girls, however, were wary of Hindley, finding her unpredictable and intimidating. Although she had been a constant day-dreamer from an early age, a childhood 'flame' recalled her as a 'real toughie, full of hiss and spit, a fighting cat'. This aggression was channelled to advantage on the school sports field, where she was captain of the netball team and an outstanding rounders player. Twice a week she went to judo lessons and was an above-average swimmer.

Most stars of sport are hero-worshipped at school, but not Hindley. She never mixed, and it was not until she was fifteen that she made her first friend, Michael Higgins, who was two years younger than her. Higgins drowned while swimming in a reservoir and Hindley, who knew she could have saved him had she been there, never forgave herself for not being present. Higgins had been a Roman Catholic and Hindley started attending the same church at which he had worshipped every Sunday. In 1958, she became a Catholic convert, taking her first Communion on November 6.

By the time Hindley met Ronnie Sinclair, who worked as a tea-blender at the Co-operative, she had become physically attractive and used extra money from baby-sitting to pay for colouring and perming her hair. However, she did not allow the baby-sitting to encroach on her dancing lessons, three nights a week, where she first met Ronnie. He soon proposed marriage and Hindley accepted, chose a diamond engagement ring, and announced a wedding date. This was hastily cancelled, however.

Hindley seemed suddenly to have discovered how to make friends, and made it obvious that she was interested in having fun with 'a more mature man'.

When she started her fourth job as a typist at Millwards Merchandise, a chemical distribution company in Gorton, Hindley was only nineteen. It was at Millwards that she fell in love with a tall, dark, brooding Scotsman who shared her office. His name was Ian Brady.

Brady was born on January 2, 1938, the illegitimate son of

Maggie Stewart, a waitress in a Glasgow tea-room. Neither he nor his mother knew the identity of his father, and he was brought up by strangers in Camden Street, a part of the disreputable Gorbals district of Glasgow.

In 1947, the family Brady grew up with moved to a council house in a better area of Glasgow, and the school he attended, Shawlands Academy, was noted for its high percentage of academic high-flyers. His obsession with horror movies earned him the nickname 'Dracula', which he loved. Even before he left school, he had broken the law, being charged with housebreaking. The magistrates, in an effort to help him, placed him on probation, but he saw this as a weakness. After jobs both as a butcher's messenger, and as a shipyard tea-boy, he made his second court appearance, on yet another housebreaking charge. On this occasion, he asked for nine other similar offences to be taken into account.

Still the magistrates were inclined to leniency, renewing his probation on the understanding that he returned to his real mother, who had married and was living in Manchester. He left Glasgow as Ian Sloane and arrived in Manchester as Ian Brady, happily embracing his mother's married name.

If the bringing together of Brady and Hindley was the outcome of some great universal master plan, it could only have been the design of the Devil's architect.

Patrick Brady, Ian's stepfather, was anxious to make his stepson feel at home. 'I wanted to be a *real* father to him,' he said: 'I knew what he'd been through. I hoped to be able to make up for everything he'd so far missed out on.' So keen was Patrick to help Ian that he tramped around Manchester's Smithfield Market to find a job for his stepson. Although Ian appeared grateful, he soon dishonoured his stepfather and was sent to Borstal for stealing. Two years later, in 1958, he was back home, working as a labourer. However, this did not last for long. Millwards Merchandise offered him a position as stock-clerk, with a salary of £600 per year. Brady took the job, and was soon to be seen in the neighbourhood dressed like a dapper man-about-town in a dark overcoat and conservative three-piece suit. No longer was he 'Dracula'. His new sob-riquet was 'Undertaker'. The first burial took place only a few weeks later.

Number 16, Wardle Brook Avenue, Hattersley, which became the monsters' lair and then their memorial, was finally demolished. Unfortunately, with its destruction only the building has gone, but its memories and its repulsive history will remain forever.

4

□□■□□

The Thames Towpath

■ EVERYTHING seemed to be happening in 1953. Undoubtedly the highlight was the coronation of Queen Elizabeth II; then soccer maestro, Stanley Matthews, finally won that elusive Cup Final winners' medal; Everest was conquered for the first time. It was also the year of 'Tarzan of the Towpath.'

In the late autumn of 1953, everyone in Britain was reading about the 'Ape Man', who wore nothing except a loincloth as he swung through the trees in parks and fields around his home, a Gurkha army knife between his teeth and an axe clasped between his feet.

In the Appeal court, later, the Lord Chief Justice, Lord Goddard, was to describe the case as 'the most brutal and horrifying before this court and any other court for years'.

Between spring and autumn, there are few more idyllic settings than beside the River Thames at Teddington, Middlesex. There is the famous weir, a cascading, foaming backdrop to so many British movies and television dramas. The weeping willows create an aura of melancholy and the river meanders lazily like a huge sleepy python. The undulating countryside of lush green fields is as neat as the gardens in this sleepy middle-class preserve. Most of the homes are 'made-to-measure': few come 'off-the-peg'. The air is sweet and the sun always shines; an illusion, of course, but no less real for all its myth. This is the Rose Garden of England; the epitome of British reserve, seclusion and security;

so safe — until May 31, 1953. From that date, Teddington was never to be quite the same again.

Summer had come early to Britain that year. The heavens were blue and clear. The sun burned down from above, and two fun-loving teenaged girls — Barbara Songhurst, a shop assistant, and Christine Reed, a factory worker — were determined to make the most of the neighbourly weather. May 31 was a Sunday, and in the afternoon the two girls decided to go for a ride on their bicycles.

Their exact movements remain a mystery, but it is likely that they headed for the river, where they might have sun-bathed, perhaps buying ice-creams, drinks and snacks at one of the numerous stalls or cafés in the vicinity. No one, later, was able to confirm a positive sighting during the afternoon.

There were lots of boats on the river: rowing-boats, canoes, larger pleasure-craft and floating gin-palaces. Portable radios throbbed to the beat of the era's top ballads. Lovers lingered, oblivious to straight-laced post-war attitudes. The newly-green trees swayed with the gentle momentum of a harmless drunk, providing fans for those spread beneath them.

It is hardly likely that Barbara, aged eighteen, and her sixteen-year-old friend, hired a boat: if they had, surely they would have been remembered? It also seems unlikely that they had a pre-arranged date. Neither of them was known to have a current boyfriend, although they were both extremely attractive.

One witness was to report having seen them swimming nude in the river at 'around 4 p.m.' while he was strolling along the Teddington towpath. During questioning, he was to say: 'I was out for a walk with my dog. From a distance, I could see two swimmers in the water. As I drew nearer, I could see that they were girls. Two piles of clothes were stacked haphazardly on the grass some ten feet from the path, and a couple of bikes were propped against a tree. The girls were giggling and waving, and I looked away. By then, I could tell they were nude. I was embarrassed. I'm married and have children of my

own. It was not the sort of behaviour one expects on a Sunday.'
He couldn't swear that the girls were Barbara and Christine,
though the odds favoured it having been them. 'I didn't look
that close,' he claimed. 'I'm not a Peeping Tom.' The police
were not prepared to take his word for that.

Beyond dispute is that by 8 p.m., Barbara and Christine
were in the company of three young men who were camping
on the river bank. The boys spent two or three hours chatting
up the girls and there was some playful petting before the girls
said that they must go home, laughing off attempts to persuade
them to stay the night. Barbara and Christine are alleged to
have agreed to return the following evening, although there is
no means of verifying this claim: if this arrangement was made,
it could well have been a ploy to enable the girls to make an
uncomplicated departure. The time they sealed their goodbyes
with an innocent kiss was 11 p.m.

When the teenagers had not returned home by midnight,
their parents became worried. The consolation was that the
girls were together. 'They won't come to any harm unless they
split up,' one father predicted confidently.

'When they're enjoying themselves, they lose track of time,'
said one mother. 'Kids can be so inconsiderate!'

They suspected and hoped that after an afternoon by the
river, Barbara and Christine had taken themselves to the
cinema, perhaps meeting friends inside — a social habit of the
Teddy-Boy Fifties.

By morning, worry had become fear. There was one last
hope: the girls had gone to an all-night party, where they had
had too much to drink, succumbed to sexual advances, and
were now recovering. Two sets of parents were literally
praying that their daughters had surrendered to temptation.
However, the odds against were high. True, they were high-
spirited teenagers, brimming with vitality, but neither Barbara
nor Christine was likely to behave in this way.

By noon on the Monday, the search for the two missing girls
had become a murder hunt. Barbara Songhurst's body had
been washed up in shallow water at Ham Fields, near

Richmond, Surrey, some three miles north of Teddington. That afternoon, an autopsy established that she had died from stab wounds and had been dead when dumped into the river. She had also been raped before the stabbing attack. The time of death was estimated at between 11 p.m. on the Sunday and 2 a.m. on the Monday.

More than two hundred police officers and soldiers were drafted into the area to scour the countryside, including forests, copses, ponds, outhouses, lakes, empty properties and disused boathouses, while naval frogmen from Portsmouth took the search under water. The towpath scenery between Teddington Lock and Richmond Bridge is very much the same today as it was then. The River Thames along that stretch is invariably in a lazy mood. It ebbs and flows without fuss, barely ruffled by the sedate, unhurried river craft which play on its lambent surface. Motor launches glide like snooty white ladies, noses high in the air. The river swells and contracts as it meanders gracefully. Richmond and its environs, renowned for their tea rooms, restaurants and pubs, are advertisements for the Good Life; people drive for miles for a drink or a meal in Richmond. It is a busy town, larger than it seems with a 160,000 population, and one foot in London and the other in the country. In summer, the blossom scatters perfume into the air. There are smart stores, a bustling High Street, countless antique shops and traffic bottlenecks, but also colonnades of trees, a royal park and a myriad of flower gardens. Richmond is a fortress within a green, pastoral wall. How incongruous that amongst all this beauty and tranquility, there must have been a bloody body in the reeds!

Scotland Yard's Chief Inspector Herbert Hannam was assigned to the case within hours of the discovery of Barbara Songhurst's body. In addition to appealing for witnesses, he warned women not to walk alone near the river until 'this sex-maniac is safely behind bars.'

The three campers who had become friendly with the girls on the Sunday night were quickly rounded up. Not unnaturally, they were treated as prime suspects, especially when they said, in separate statements, that Barbara and Christine had been with them until eleven o'clock. 'The postmortem indicates that she could have been killed at eleven,' Hannam reminded his men. Campers usually have knives and these lads were no exception. Three knives, similar to those used by scouts, were taken from their tent and submitted to every conceivable forensic test known to science detection in those times. The outcome was a lab report that excluded the campers' knives from the investigation. This did not automatically exonerate the young men, however, but it helped. Hannam continually pressed to know whether sexual intercourse had taken place with the girls, and if they had been harassed and detained against their will. These suggestions were dismissed by the campers. Hannam wanted to establish whether rape or murder had occurred because of sexual frustration, but they vehemently denied this, and all knowledge of where Christine Reed was now.

Another group of campers had heard screaming 'at approximately 11 p.m.'. This evidence seemed further to incriminate the youths who admitted having been with the girls for 'two hours or more'. But the same day another witness reported seeing a man riding a woman's bicycle at 11.20 p.m., along the towpath at Teddington, on the night in question. Could that have been the killer making his escape on the bicycle of one of his victims? It seemed very likely to Hannam, although he was determined to keep an open mind.

Forensic tests at the site where the campers had pitched their tent were negative: no bloodstains nor grass trodden and trampled in such a way as to indicate a struggle. Neither were there scratch marks nor bruises on the faces or hands of the suspects.

On the Tuesday, frogmen plucked Barbara Songhurst's bicycle from the river about a mile from the spot where they had spent the evening. The other bike remained missing, adding credibility to the theory that the killer had left on Christine's bicycle. If so, that would exonerate the three young campers.

The immediate task was to find Christine Reed's body. Although Hannam, in consideration for the feelings of relatives of the missing girl, did not say so publicly, he had given up all hope of finding Christine alive. He felt certain that this was a case of double murder; probably double rape, as well too.

During every hour of daylight the frogmen continued to drag the river, while uniformed policemen, drafted from several forces of the Home Counties, combed every inch of countryside for miles around. The police were not on their own: they were joined by military volunteers and hundreds of members of the public — especially parents who had daughters.

Recently, I hired a boat in Richmond and rowed upstream under the bridge. A racing eight passed me in the opposite direction, more graceful than a swan, travelling fast but without fury, cohesive strength generated in meticulous timing, all spurred on by a diminutive, slumped figure in the stern, the baby-faced cox. A punt had come to rest beside the bank, partially camouflaged by reeds. A young man and his girl lay prostrate, a knot of arms and legs, oblivious to a transient audience.

I rowed on, following the course of the police launch on June 6, 1953. The frogmen had moved north along the river, following the flow, and a number of police launches maundered up and down, the officers on board using binoculars to expand their horizons. Although the search had to be maintained on all fronts, Hannam was certain that Christine Reed's body would be found in the Thames.

Richmond Bridge receded, seeming to lower itself into the murky water, which acted like blotting paper, soaking up sound. There was something eerie about that vacuum, even at mid-day.

I turned to check my bearings. Floating a few feet ahead of me was a log, mostly submerged, and I shuddered to think that Christine Reed's body was spotted from a police launch in this exact stretch of river, one mile upstream from Richmond Bridge.

Christine Reed had been knifed in the chest and back, and there were two fractures to her skull. She had also been raped, after death. Two days later, an appeal to the public was made by the Assistant Commissioner of the Metropolitan Police, Ronald Howe, who referred to the killer as 'one of the worst sex-maniacs on record'. In a statement to the Press, he said: 'It could be that someone is hiding this man. If so, just consider the consequences. Perhaps you are suspicious about your husband, son, or next door neighbour: maybe he returned home late on May 31 on a woman's bicycle, or there was blood on his clothes. If this man is not found quickly, there is the danger that he will kill again. Is that something you could live with on your conscience?

The search of the Thames continued. Although both bodies had now been recovered, there was a deficiency of clues. One bicycle was still missing, and there was no sign either of the knife, or the other weapon which had been used to inflict the head wounds on Christine Reed. Moreover, the only sighting of a suspect had been the man riding a woman's bicycle, and the witness was unable to provide a worthwhile description. For a month, frogmen dragged every inch of the river between Teddington and Richmond's upper reaches, but without success. Hannam, meanwhile, had been going through the files of every known sex offender in the area. One by one they were picked up and interrogated. Hundreds of statements were taken, checked and filed.

As June came to an end in a blaze of glorious sunshine, the police seemed no closer to a breakthrough than on the first day of the investigation. Experience convinced Hannam that the double killer and rapist must be someone with at least one previous conviction for a sex crime. On June 29, a detective at Richmond Police Station drew Hannam's attention to the criminal-record file of Alfred Charles Whiteway, a labourer, who had just been arrested in connection with the assault of a woman and a girl in Oxshott Woods, Surrey, on May 24. The fourteen-year-old child had also been raped and injured with an axe. Whiteway had several previous convictions, but all of them for theft. Hannam was not hopeful as he stepped into Whiteway's cell at Richmond Police Station. The superintendent asked Whiteway to account for his movements on the night of May 31. The suspect, aged twenty-two, explained that he had spent the evening with his wife, Cherry, who was three years younger than himself. At 11.30 p.m., he had left his wife to cycle to No. 24, Sydney Road, Teddington, where he was living with his parents. 'Why are you separated from your wife?' Hannam enquired.

'Because there's not enough room for us all to live together,' Whiteway replied. Cherry lived with their two children in one room in Wandsworth. 'We're looking for somewhere bigger, but we don't have the money,' he said.

The introduction of Sydney Road, Teddington, touched a nerve of excitement in Hannam. Until nine years ago, Barbara Songhurst had lived at No. 9, Sydney Road.

'Does the name Barbara Songhurst mean anything to you?' Hannam probed.

After a moment's thought, Whiteway answered: 'Yes. She lived in our road, when she was a little girl. I haven't seen her, though, since she went away a long time ago.'

A search of Whiteway's parents' home produced an amazing cache of knives, including a Gurkha kukri knife. And in a top drawer in Whiteway's bedroom, the police found a pair of loin-cloth 'Tarzan' shorts. When confronted with this haul, Whiteway admitted that they belonged to him, explaining that knife-throwing was his passion. When asked about the loincloth, he said: 'Oh, that's for when I mess about in the trees, playing "Tarzan".' It also transpired that he had a passion for physical fitness.

Hannam wanted to know more about this man. Murder Squad detectives from Scotland Yard, working in pairs, were despatched into the Teddington area to build up a comprehensive picture of the background and personality of Whiteway. One female witness described seeing a man naked, except for 'swimming trunks, something like that, around his waist and a knife in his mouth', swinging on the branch of a tree beside the river one evening. 'That was probably me,' admitted Whiteway, when this evidence was put to him. 'I do it for exercise.'

Cherry Whiteway confirmed that her husband had been with her on the Sunday night in question, but she was uncertain about the exact time he left. 'It could have been 11.20; it might have been earlier.' Clearly there had been no collusion between husband and wife in concocting an alibi.

Roy Tarp, a teacher, came forward to testify that a month before the double murder, he had seen Whiteway throwing knives at a tree beside the Teddington towpath. 'It was just target practice,' Whiteway explained. When asked for what, he replied: 'Nothing. I was just messing. It's fun.'

The soles of the shoes which Whiteway had been wearing on May 31 appeared to have been scrubbed, but a few bloodstains remained. However, there was not enough for a positive match to be made: forensic medicine was not yet sufficiently advanced. Hannam believed he had found his man, but the case against Whiteway was a porous one. Many gaps had to be filled. For example, if Whiteway was cycling home on the night of the murder, what did he do with Christine Reed's bicycle? Why should he throw one in the river and not the other? How could he have managed two bikes on his own without being noticed?

In any event, Whiteway was detained for the alleged offences in Oxshott Woods, although by now he had become the one and only suspect for the towpath crimes. The breakthrough Hannam had been hoping for came on July 15 in a manner so sensational that it was to blight the career of one policeman, and cast a shadow at the Old Bailey over the entire case for the prosecution. A constable at Kingston Police Station gave an axe to one of his colleagues, sheepishly explaining that it had been left under the seat of a patrol car. He had found the axe in the car on June 18, the day after Whiteway had been arrested on Oxshott Heath, and the police car was the same one in which Whiteway had been driven from the Heath to Kingston Police Station. However, the constable had kept the axe for almost a month, having taken it home for the purpose of chopping wood.

On July 30, Whiteway made two statements at Scotland Yard. In the second, he was alleged to have confessed with the words: 'It's all up. You know bloody well I done it, eh! I'm mental.' But when he was charged on August 20, he said categorically: 'I deny the charges.' At the trial, which began on October 26, Peter Rawlinson (later to become Sir Peter and Attorney General in the Heath Government) accused Hannam of forging Whiteway's confession. Criminologists described the courtroom confrontation as the most savage ever witnessed in a British trial. No one could recall such a scathing attack by counsel on the personal credibility of a senior Scotland Yard officer. Nevertheless, the jury took a mere forty-seven minutes to reach a unanimous verdict. The Court of Appeal was no less decisive. The case for the prosecution rested upon the axe, which Christmas Humphreys, representing the Crown, argued had been used by Whiteway to cause the injuries to Christine Reed's skull.

The final death venue in this lurid story was Wandsworth Prison in south London. One of the prison officers assigned to Whiteway's condemned cell in Death Row talked to me about those last agonizing weeks in Whiteway's life, providing a unique insight into the grim preparation of a man for the scaffold. 'He didn't seem to be in any state of shock when he came from the Old Bailey, having just been sentenced to hang,' said Sid Baggett. 'I think I was more nervous than he was. I'd never been chosen for death duty before. I wasn't sure whether I could handle it. I said: "Hello, Alfie. I'm Sid. I hope we're going to get along." He was stretched on his bed, his hands clasped behind his head. Very slowly he uncoiled and rose to his full height. I knew immediately why he was called "Tarzan". He wasn't too tall, but he was built like a tank. I thought to myself: *I'm never going to turn my back on you.* Alfie moved towards me ponderously and shook my hand. Our eyes locked and for a couple of seconds we measured one another. He tested my grip and I held my own as he applied pressure. It was Alfie who broke the lock, smiling mysteriously and saying: "Okay, do you play cards?" I replied: "Whenever you're ready." He said: "We'll start tomorrow. I enjoy a game of cards — as long as I win." The smile had gone and I could tell he wasn't joking.'

The cell was remarkably large, its size surprising even Baggett. Two walls had been demolished and three cells had been converted into one; there was a bathroom and lavatory next door. In all, there were six cells and the same number of bathrooms on Death Row, which was fully occupied that Christmas.

Baggett continued his story: 'During my first night on duty, the chief screw took me and my partner aside, telling us: "I never want to see daylight between you and your prisoner. When he eats, you stand by his side, watching every mouthful until it's gone down. When he has a visitor, you flank him. When he goes to the lavatory, you hold his hand. Your job is to get him to the rope alive and well." There was tremendous emphasis placed on the health of a condemned prisoner. The attitude was that a condemned man should go to his death in the pink of health, blooming if possible.'

Prisoners on Death Row were not allowed any personal belongings, including family photographs: Whiteway had two young daughters. Every day he received letters from his wife, Cherry, and his mother, but he had to read them in front of his guards. The moment he had finished reading, the letters were confiscated, to prevent him from using them to choke himself.

'About three o'clock in the morning on the first night, Alfie began to stir,' the ex-prison officer recalled. 'As he lay, still fast asleep, he began opening and clenching his fists. At one point, his knuckles went white and his nails cut into the flesh of his palms. I was amazed by the size of his hands. They were goal-keeper's hands — heavy white slabs of concrete, out of proportion to the rest of his body.

'One of us shaved him every morning. We'd have lost our jobs if we'd given him the opportunity to cut his throat. He wasn't even allowed to flush the toilet: we had to do that for him. It was against the rules for a condemned man to be seen by another prisoner, under any circumstances. When Alfie took his daily exercise in the yard, the other prisoners had to be locked up and it was an offence for them to stand, at that time, at the window.

'Contrary to legend, there was no special food for a condemned man. He took his chance along with the rest. Breakfast consisted of porridge, one rasher of bacon, a dry bread roll — no butter or margarine — and a mug of tea. All cutlery was plastic and was removed from the cell the moment he'd finished eating. Alfie ate well that first morning and I asked him how he was feeling. He replied: "Never better."

'When he prowled around the cell, he was like a restless bear. One day he stood behind his chair and wrapped his arms around his back. Slowly he lowered his head, his eyes narrowing. I wondered what the hell he was up to. I nudged my partner and he braced himself. Alfie's mouth opened, revealing a perfect set of pearly white teeth. The next moment, he had the chair between his teeth and he was lifting it from the floor, at least four feet off the ground. Three times he strutted around the cell with the chair in his mouth, swinging it a couple of times. He was the strongest young fella I'd ever come across, and I'd seen a few in my time in the Second World War in North Africa, Italy and Europe.

'Naturally, Alfie's "Tarzan" tricks gave me plenty to write about in the Occurrence Book. Big, he was, but never violent. There was not one outburst. He kept everything inside. I often wondered what he was thinking, what he had done with his life, if anything, but he always changed the subject. He wasn't secretive, just silent. A senior screw, without realizing what he was saying, said to me one day: "This experience will make a man of him!" That sort of comment wasn't uncommon: it was all very bizarre and unreal. Although I had no sympathy for Alfie, a relationship did mature between us. It was unavoidable: we were thrown together for eight hours every

Pembridge Court Hotel, where Neville Heath killed so brutally.

Pembridge Gardens, where Neville Heath made his escape.

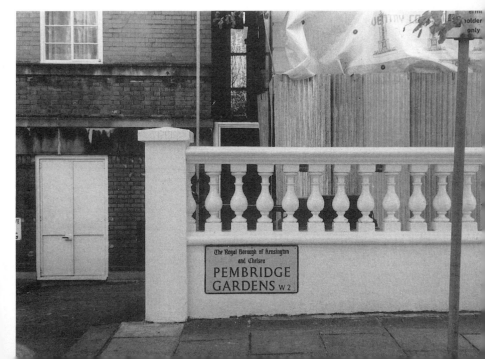

The beauty spot in Branksome Dene Chine, Dorset, where Doreen Marshall's body was found.

Doreen Marshall had afternoon tea and cucumber sandwiches at the Tollard Royal Hotel, Bournemouth, with a handsome man just hours before he mutilated her. The Hotel is now a block of luxury flats and has been re-named Tollard Court.

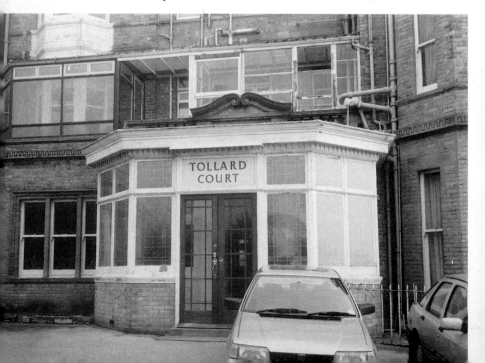

The *Jack the Ripper* pub in London's Commercial Street, which has now reverted to its original name, *The Ten Bells*. (Photograph by Peter Underwood, F.R.S.A. from *Jack the Ripper – One Hundred Years of Mystery*.)

Wardle Brook Avenue, shortly before demolition, where Ian Brady and Myra Hindley claimed their final victim. Nobody was able to live there for long following the murder.

The towpath where Barbara Songhurst and Christine Reed met their killer.

Rural bliss, but not for Christine Reed. This is where her floating body came to rest.

Burgate House, here a family was massacred.

The exact spot in the A6 lay-by at Deadman's Hill where a young man and woman were cut down in their prime.

No. 105, Onslow Square, the scene of Detective Sergeant Raymond Purdy's murder.

The Blind Beggar pub in London's tough East End, where George Cornell was gunned down at the bar.

No. 1, Evering Road, Stoke Newington. 'Jack the Hat' McVitie was stabbed to death in the basement.

The historic *Magdala Tavern* in Hampstead, scene of the shooting of David Blakely by Ruth Ellis.

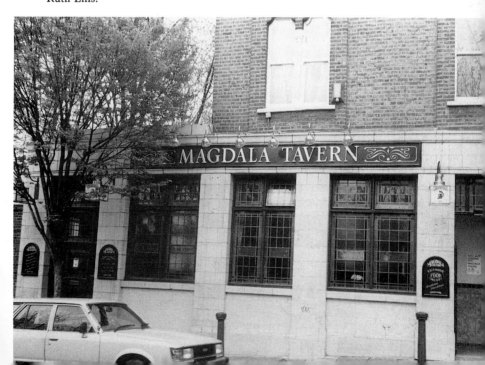

No. 195, Melrose Avenue, where Dennis Nilsen's killing spree began.

No. 23, Cranley Gardens, the last home of mass murderer Dennis Nilsen.

day in a small room, so it was to the advantage of us both to rub along with as little friction as possible.

'I also had to admire him — the way a soldier can be respected by the enemy. I saw thousands of men die in war. None of them had time to think about their death. It happened in an atom of time. But Alfie had the days and the nights, over a period of weeks, to contemplate that noose at the end of the rope. He didn't once beg for mercy. He didn't even plead with the priest. He seemed to take each day in his stride, fighting the fear internally. I'll never know what bargain he struck with himself, but it must have had something to do with not allowing the world to see any show of weakness.

'When I was on day duty, I would see his wife and kids during visiting. We would take Alfie to a special room. His wife would be the other side of a double-plated glass panel and several layers of wire mesh. Nothing, except words, was permitted to pass between them. They were forbidden to touch, which was impossible, anyhow, because they were effectively in separate rooms. The first time, the conversation started: "You're looking well, Alfie." "So do you. You look really swell, luv. I'm missing you." "Me you. Are they treating you all right?" "It's all right here. A bit boring, but not bad, considering."

'Cherry mentioned that she was praying for him every night, but he didn't respond to that. If Alfie did any praying when I was with him, he kept it very private. I don't recall him once asking for the chaplain, not even in the last hours. I've a feeling he was determined to die without betraying himself.

'Every time I used to offer him sweets, he used to say: "Don't tempt me. Don't you know how bad sweets are for your teeth?" Alfie had less than a month to live and he was worried about sugar rotting his teeth! He was also finicky about food. He refused to eat fat and most fried stuff because he was afraid of putting on weight and losing his athletic figure. A part of Alfie continued to plan for a future he didn't have: apparently that was a feature of the unreality of life in the death cell.

'Alfie was also a non-smoker. We often offered him a smoke, thinking it might help him to relax, but that really annoyed him. He'd say: "Are you trying to give me lung cancer?" At night I used to tell him bedtime stories. His eyes were truly wide with wonder when I told him about my army days. He never wanted me to finish and he'd say: "Did that really happen, Sid? Was it really like that?" When I ran out of steam, I'd tell him: "No more tonight, Alfie, but I'll prepare a good one for you tomorrow." And he'd press: "You promise?" He would look forward eagerly to the next night, seemingly forgetting that it would bring him one day nearer the hangman.

'After story-time, I would always suggest a game of cards. We tried to keep him awake as long as possible because the night shift could be a long drag. We allowed Alfie to choose the game. He was a poker fan. We played for make-believe stakes. One night I lost Wandsworth Prison to him. He still owes me Buckingham Palace. Quite suddenly he'd ask the time: he wasn't allowed a watch. I'd reply: "What's it matter, Alfie? You've nowhere to go." But that wouldn't pacify him. He'd complain that he was missing his beauty sleep; that he was becoming so unfit.

'Frequently I'd bump into Cherry Whiteway in the street. Usually she'd be pushing her two little kids. She'd come up to me, all smiles: "Hello, Mr Baggett. How's my Alfie today?" Then she'd add something like: "I'm very grateful to you for looking after him so well. Alfie usually finds it difficult to get on with strangers, but he certainly seems to have taken to you." We waved goodbye to each other and anyone watching must have believed we were long-standing friends, or even family.'

The execution date by then had been fixed for December 22 at 9 a.m.

The catering staff at Wandsworth Prison were preparing to serve several hundred Christmas dinners on the 25th, and Alfie Whiteway's name had been struck off the list.

Sid Baggett used to have a drink most nights in a pub close to the prison. Before leaving, he would buy a packet of crisps for

Alfie, who always appreciated this and once said: "They bring back memories of nights out with the missis."

There was an unfortunate incident one evening while Alfie was in his bathroom with Sid. On the opposite side of the wall, another condemned prisoner was in his washroom with his warder and every word of their conversation could be heard. A part of it went thus: "How far will I drop?" "Far enough! You'll find out when the rope snaps your neck. No need to worry your fat head about those details."

Baggett felt ashamed. 'That particular screw was really crude and I felt a pang of sympathy for Alfie who couldn't avoid hearing. It didn't dampen his appetite, though. He ate his supper and all his meals the next day.'

Whiteway's appeal was heard and dismissed on December 7.

During their weeks together, Baggett often asked Alfie what he had done with the missing bicycle. 'I hadn't been put up to it by the police,' said Baggett. 'I was genuinely intrigued. There were loose ends that bothered me. But he would never answer. He always changed the subject when I tried to talk about the case. But I did once ask him straight out if he did it, explaining to him: "It would help me if I knew. I'd feel better if you told me." All he said was: "Tell me another story, Sid. One of your Hong Kong stories."

'More than any, he loved the tales about my army days in Hong Kong, particularly concerning the brothels for the married servicemen. "Were they really like that?" he'd ask, eyes swelling. "You're so lucky, Sid. You've done so much. I've done nothing. I never shall now, shall I?"

'Then his face suddenly lit up and he said: "But I'm going to die before you, Sid!" It was said with a sort of gush of triumph, as if he was saying: "*There, Sid, I'm going to beat you at something.*"

'A couple of days before the execution, we moved cells, putting Alfie directly next to what was known as the 'topping shed'. Even then, he still seemed to be eating and sleeping well.

That week we'd learned who would be doing the final death-watch, the last night shift, sitting with the prisoner through his final hours and then leading him to the noose. I'd drawn the short straw. I nearly died at the thought of it, although it was something, of course, I'd considered right from the very start — though always hoping it would be someone else.

'I'd seen thousands of young men slaughtered in war, but somehow this was very different. We were going to kill a kid I'd been living with for something like seven weeks. The possibility of putting a rope around the neck of the wrong man or woman troubles me; that's why I wanted Alfie to tell me he'd done it, to satisfy my own conscience, but he wouldn't give me that peace. And even today, I still wonder: those loose ends bother me.

'Alfie's wife continued to visit. I'll never forget the last visit of his mother: that was traumatic. "Be a good boy in heaven, won't you, Alfie?" she wept. He was saying: "Try to have a swell Christmas, Mum. Don't let this spoil Christmas Day for you. Do you think He'll have me in heaven?" It was very distressing, but I'd been trained not to have sympathy for prisoners.

'Cherry's last visit was on the afternoon before the execution. Still they weren't allowed to touch. Their final kisses were blown through the glass and wire panel. The little girls were there, too, not realizing the poignance of their last wave to Daddy.

'That night, we played cards again. I was in a lather under my uniform. Alfie must have slipped into sleep around two o'clock, but he was awake early. The usual morning routines were observed. Alfie washed and went to the toilet, then I shaved him. He must have been dreading seeing first light peeping through the bars: I know I was. Not once did he ask me the time that final morning. Breakfast came on a tray, no earlier than usual and nothing special about it; porridge with all the traditional lumps. And for the first time, Alfie wasn't interested in his food. He pushed it aside, without comment.

'I kept looking at my watch. The only ticking I could hear was coming from my heart. It was kicking my ribs. Alfie was very subdued, but he wasn't pacing. He just sat, waiting quietly.

'Contrary to popular belief, there was never a procession from the condemned cell to the noose, led by the chaplain and governor. It was just Alfie, me and my partner. This is how it happened.

'Just before nine, the door to the 'topping shed' swung open and the chief screw marched in like a sergeant-major, saying firmly: "Right, lad, let's have you."

I said to Alfie: "It's time to go, son. Are you okay?" He didn't reply. He stood up and I positioned myself one side of him, my partner the other side. That's when his legs started to go. I gripped him by the arm. Suddenly he was crying. "This is no time for bawling, lad," said the chief screw. "Let's see what you're made of."

'Inside the 'topping shed' were two hangmen, the governor, his deputy, the chaplain, and two of the biggest screws I've ever seen in all my life. The giant screws strapped Alfie's hands behind his back and the hangman slipped a hood over his head. As Alfie began to sob and shudder, the chaplain took a step forward, but Alfie was disappearing through the floor.

'It all happened so incredibly quickly. The chaplain said to me afterwards: "I was going to try to comfort him, but before I had a chance to put a hand on his shoulders, he was dropping. I didn't even have time to say a prayer for him."

'By then, I was ready for the Christmas holiday.'

Some people would say that this is a story of three murders, the first two beside the River Thames at Teddington, and the third in Wandsworth Prison.

5

□□■□□

Burgate House

■ BURGATE House is best approached from the River
Avon. As I stood on those gently sloping banks, looking across
to the softly rolling meadows, I thought of Joseph Cleaver
fishing for eels. How he had enjoyed his sport — especially
angling and horse-racing. He had also loved his food and eels
were one of his favourite dishes, especially when he had caught
them himself. But those happy days were over and even
though the sun was shining, there was a cloud over the whole
estate that bore no relation to the weather.

I turned my back on the teeming river and started towards
the house itself, a stucco building with old-fashioned, blue-
painted windows; a decorous, coy mansion, hiding, it seemed,
behind a proliferation of trees and bushes. Even in this age of
aggressive competition, the serene and leisurely game of
croquet was played regularly on the verdant lawns, until the
night of September 1, 1986. From that night, Burgate House,
in the English picture-postcard town of Fordingbridge,
Hampshire, has inherited a legacy no less odious than that of
Roman Polanski's house in Los Angeles, where Charles
Manson and his evil disciples massacred the pregnant actress
Sharon Tate and all her dinner guests.

The front door is made of sturdy oak, the upper half a
montage of coloured glass. On the morning of September 2,
1986, the local milkman had left three pints at five o'clock on
the gravel path outside, unaware of the horror within.

Two hours later, the postman, Roy Gaunt, arrived. The

front door was ajar and he tossed the mail on to the floor in the hallway, next to a golfbag, a shooting-stick and a collection of umbrellas in a rack under a small window, over which short-length curtains were still drawn. Even he did not sense the smell of death, and disappeared on his bicycle, whistling as he went about his usual morning routine.

Next on the scene was Darren Andrews, a youth who had volunteered to undertake maintenance work on the Cleavers' Hollywood-style swimming pool. When all his knocks and calls went unanswered, he hurried home to tell his mother, Maureen Andrews, that he was 'worried'.

Darren was followed to Burgate House by the newsagent, George Biffen, who placed the *Times* and *The Daily Telegraph* on the floor, just inside the front door, beside the post.

Nellie Taylor had been a friend of the Cleaver family for something like fifty years. It was just before ten o'clock when she and the gardener, Eddie Stubbings, approached Burgate House and noticed that a number of windows had been smashed. There was also external evidence that there had been a fire upstairs. Their advance to the mansion was completed at a trot.

Fifteen minutes later, the elderly couple were standing in front of Police Constable Roger Carter at Fordingbridge Police Station, breathless, Mr Stubbings almost choking on his words: 'I want to report a murder.'

'It didn't sound real,' the Constable recalled. 'It seemed like something you hear on TV; the sort of stuff from which fiction is made.'

Unfortunately, it was not make-believe. Mr Stubbings and Mrs Taylor had found the body of Wendy Cleaver, the daughter-in-law of millionaires Joseph and Hilda Cleaver. At that time, they didn't realize that they had seen only a small part of the horror that was to unfold.

Still doubting the veracity of what he had just heard, Constable Carter set off for Burgate House, about three miles away, closely followed by policewoman Jan Bulfield, with Mr Stubbings and Mrs Taylor bringing up the rear.

I stood in the hallway at Burgate House and tried to picture the scene on the morning that the two police officers pushed back the already half-open front door, immediately almost tripping over the Cleavers' pet poodle. The poor animal had been battered to death.

Leading the way, Constable Carter had gone up the staircase three stairs at a time, noticing the black burn-holes in the red-and-blue carpets. Bulfield had been close behind him, drawing attention to all the firelighters littering the floors. As I cautiously made my way towards the bedroom that served as Satan's chamber of horrors, the charged atmosphere remained, all those months after the trial.

I mounted the first flight of twelve steps very deliberately, all the time thinking of those hapless people, who had been torn from the dining table and forced up these very stairs. Possibly they had groped for the handrail on the right-hand side, passing the gilt-framed paintings on the walls, the whole ghastly nightmare illuminated by the harsh brightness of the chandelier lights.

On reaching the landing, the officers had spotted a door wedged open by a jewellery-box. They did not know it at the time, but they were about to enter the master bedroom, where Joseph had slept for thirty years or more with his wife, Hilda, whom he cherished, and where they had died together. Their nurse, Margaret Murphy, died with them as well as the 'butchers' who had perpetrated this atrocity.

The chill of fear swept through me as I vacillated on the threshold, half expecting that the bodies would still be there — one in a chair, another on the bed and a third on the floor.

Constable Carter told the Press: 'I could see one body in a chair. The body had injuries to the head and I thought, at first, it was a man because of the trousers. Later, of course, I discovered it was a woman. Lying in the middle of the bed was Mr Cleaver and there was another badly burned body down by the side of the bed. There was still a lot of smoke in the room, just hanging there. A couple of fires were still burning. The bed and one of the chairs were still alight.'

At the other end of the landing is the bedroom in which Constable Carter discovered Wendy Cleaver, lying on her back with her hands tied behind her. She was naked except for a slip. There was a black ribbon noose fastened around her neck and she had been set alight. 'Rigor mortis had set in,' Carter later recalled.

As the officers stumbled across new bodies in almost every room, two dachshunds scampered over the house in blind panic. Jan Bulfield, who described the mayhem over her radio to police headquarters, decided to place herself on guard outside the house to prevent unauthorized people wandering on to the estate and possibly tampering with evidence. It was on her way out that she noticed that the poodle, Tina, had not only been battered to death, but that one of her eyes had been gouged out.

Not until the arrival of the fire brigade was the fifth and final body found — that of Tom Cleaver, Wendy's husband. He had died under the washbasin in the bathroom, which was linked by a joining door to the master bedroom. 'It was so hot in there because the house is made of solid concrete,' policewoman Bulfield remembered. 'It was like a kiln in there, unbearable... unforgettable.'

What had happened?

Let us start in the dining room, because that is where, unknowingly, five innocent people had sat down to their last supper. The Cleavers were the kind of family who always dined at eight o'clock sharp. Dinner was taken seriously, old customs religiously observed. The men wore suits, the women decorated themselves in their best jewellery and finest dresses. Conversation and wine would have been of vintage quality. Old England may have died elsewhere, but in Burgate House, on the fringe of the New Forest, the values of the Empire lived on until that wretched night when they were snuffed out by three evil men with nothing but malice, greed, envy and lust in their hearts.

The expensive silverware would have been glittering under the diamond-cluster chandeliers, and the candles doubtlessly helped to soften the atmosphere. The family's fierce patriotism was reflected in the photographs on the dining-room walls of the Prince and Princess of Wales and their children. The Cleavers were great believers in The Family.

Wendy Cleaver had gone to Burgate House to care for her in-laws while the elderly couple looked for a new home-help. Joseph and Hilda Cleaver were in their eighties and their last housekeeper had had to leave because her husband physically abused her. Her husband was called George Stephenson and was also employed as the handyman. Wendy's husband, Tom, who owned a catering company and a chain of wine bars, had also joined the family gathering that evening. By eight o'clock, they were all seated around the long, elegant Regency table. Naturally, Joseph placed himself at the head of the table. Facing him was his son, Tom, aged forty-nine. Under the Royal pictures were Hilda and Wendy, who was forty-six and vivacious. Opposite them was the live-in nurse, Margaret Murphy, a sprightly seventy-year-old.

The previous day, fresh vegetables and melons had been delivered by greengrocer Dan Lennan. On the morning after the final supper, with everyone in the house dead, cooked but uneaten broccoli, courgettes and carrots remained in the silver dishes in which they had been served. There was also a bowl of untouched fruit. A recently sharpened carving knife lay naked on a serving napkin beside Joseph Cleaver's place. Even at eighty-two, he had insisted on carrying out all the duties of the head of the family.

Dinner was never rushed, especially when it was something of a family reunion. Good conversation, good food and good wine were not things to be hurried. Everyone at that table was a connoisseur of Good Living. There is no means of telling what they talked about, and if business concentrated their minds, it would not have been for too long: Joseph was a great believer in making sure that work kept its place. He had founded the immensely successful publishing company, Cleaver-Hume Press, with his partner Harry Hume, specializing in correspondence courses. Although he had refused to retire, in the latter years of his life much of the day-to-day running of the business had been entrusted to one of his three sons, Jimmy, who was an accountant. It's much more likely that sport and recreational subjects had helped them to linger over the game soup and roast beef. Joseph was such a fan of racing that in his heyday he had owned a string of horses. In 1948, he had two runners in the Grand National — Some Chicken and Sen Toi. Some Chicken, partnered by Davy Jones, finished fifth. During their golden years until they were about seventy, the couple never missed a day of Royal Ascot.

Tom and Wendy owned a flat at Cheltenham and had a reputation for their lavish parties during the Cheltenham Festival Meeting. Greyhound racing was another of Joseph's many sporting loves, dating back to the Thirties. His biggest triumph on the dog tracks came in 1938, when two greyhounds he owned finished first and second in the Grand National at the White City. Juvenile Classic won the race in a new record time of 30.36 seconds, with Bay Moon breathing down its neck, a mere half-a-length away. Juvenile Classic and its brother, Junior Classic, earned something in the region of £7,000 in prize money for Joseph Cleaver — which was a large sum in the Thirties. Those heady days tended to dominate the dialogue whenever Joseph and his wife indulged in nostalgia.

But I digress. Let us return to the evening of September 1, 1986. There they were, the five of them, replete and fortified, pausing before fruit and the selection of cheeses. Picture the splendour of it all, the sumptuous luxury and opulence. How safe they must have felt in their idyllic backwater retreat. So safe that it did not occur to them to lock their doors until retiring for bed.

The countdown to massacre, begun days ago, now reached its climax. The door flew open and in burst three raiders, all wearing stocking masks and wielding pickaxe handles. In order to warn the family what would happen if they did not co-operate and hand over all their jewels and cash, the intruders tortured the poodle to death.

All five diners were forced upstairs, including Hilda, who was partially paralysed, having suffered a severe stroke. Suddenly the telephone began to ring and one of the gang answered it. The caller was Jason Cleaver, the twenty-one-year-old son of Thomas and Wendy, who wanted to speak with his father. Jason was told that it was impossible for his father to come to the telephone and found himself cut off. Jason called again, not satisfied with the answer, and demanded to know to whom he was speaking. Once more his request was denied, by which time Jason was becoming very suspicious and reconnected himself immediately.

Realizing that Jason was likely to alert the police if his mind was not put at rest, the thugs marched Tom Cleaver to the telephone and ordered him to tell his son that Wendy was in bed with 'flu, but that there was no cause for alarm. 'I must get back to your mother,' Tom had said.

Four of the victims were pushed into the master bedroom, where they were bound and gagged, before being doused with petrol and set alight. For Wendy, however, the end was to be even more harrowing. She was dragged to a separate bedroom, where, threatened with a loaded shotgun, she was raped by each of the intruders. When they had finished, a noose was slipped around her neck and tightened for a pitiless five minutes, until they were certain no flicker of life could possibly be left in her.

Firelighters were tossed among the other trussed-up members of the household, but death was not instantaneous for them either. Firemen believed they could have taken up to half an hour to die. Tom Cleaver managed partially to free himself and crawl to the bathroom, overcome by fumes. All the bodies were so badly burned that the police had to label them A, B, C, D and E. Later, Wendy Cleaver was identified by her distinctive jewellery, which her tormentors had not bothered to steal, despite its value. Margaret Murphy was pinpointed through the wired corset she was wearing. The caliper fitted to one of Hilda Cleaver's legs was another vital clue. Thomas's semi-artificial leg was a means of differentiating between the men. It was a gruesome job for the police and firemen.

Chief Superintendent Alan Wheeler described the killings as 'bad as you are likely to find'. Drawers had been ransacked. One of the gang had helped himself to half-a-pint of milk, leaving the bottle near the front door. Someone else had sampled the wine. Untouched, however, were the priceless paintings on the walls beside the imposing staircase. They had also left Joseph's study alone: his den, which was awash with files and business papers, wedding photographs and glass cases containing the pride of his fishing catches.

Fortunately for the police, the killers left clues that were obvious to the expert eye. By six o'clock on the first evening of the investigation, the Hampshire police were making full use of their sophisticated Holmes Computer on a recently installed Honeywell, enabling them to check and cross-match information on a screen. In fact, there was no one in the Hampshire force qualified to operate the complicated machine, so a six-man team from Bedfordshire had been despatched to Winchester early that afternoon. The Bedfordshire officers had just completed their training course on the Holmes Computer.

Progress was being made rapidly. On hearing about the horrific crimes, a Fiona Stephenson had gone to Scotland Yard to report that she and her husband George, had, until recently, been employed at Burgate House. She also reported that her husband, George Stephenson, had been sacked after he had assaulted her and that they had separated. In her statement, Mrs Stephenson said that she had married her husband after a two-week 'whirlwind romance', during which time she had been swept off her feet.

George Francis Stephenson, the son of an army sergeant major, was born in Bishop Auckland, County Durham, on September 7, 1951, and was educated at a German boarding school during one of his father's overseas postings. His first job was at the Easington Colliery in Peterlee, but that did not last long: his family moved to Coventry in December, 1968. From then on, he was in and out of work, constantly changing jobs, but achieving a reputation as something of a Svengali. All the girls loved him. When he was twenty, he married Julia Rose Gossage, two years his junior, at the Parish Church of Stoke St Michael, Coventry, on October 23, 1971. Their daughter, Rachel, was born six months later, but the marriage was already running out of steam. In all, it lasted four years.

Stephenson was a building jobber in London when he met Fiona, a freelance marketing executive. Fifteen days later, they were married, on September 6, 1985, at Greenwich Registry Office, but by the summer of 1986, they were living with friends in Bournemouth, Dorset.

In everything he did, Stephenson had to be the boss. In her statement, Fiona catalogued the violence and sexual abuse to which she had been subjected by her husband since the first day of their turbulent marriage. On the New Year's Eve, just three months after their wedding, they were lying side by side on the bed, apparently blissfully happy. Suddenly he produced a knife, which he waved in front of her face, ordering her to stand, then sit, then stand, then sit, and so on. 'Prepare to die!' he is alleged to have roared at his wife insanely. She regaled the police with many other similar stories: at a stag party, for example, he tied a scarf around her neck until she blacked out.

Just after they arrived in Bournemouth, Stephenson read an advertisement in the local evening newspaper for a handyman and housekeeper. Stephenson and his wife applied, and they were invited to Burgate House for an interview. Joseph Cleaver, who was by nature a cautious man, was completely duped by Stephenson's veneer of charm and probity. So much so that for the first time in his life, he did not ask for references; a fatal mistake.

The police, however, were more thorough. Their records showed that Stephenson was an ex-Borstal inmate. When he was nineteen, he had been convicted at Coventry Quarter Sessions of burglary, deception and possessing dangerous drugs. In 1980, at Cambridge Crown Court, he was jailed for two-and-a-half years after being found in possession of a Luger pistol, a stick of gelignite and a tear-gas gun which he had fired in the face of a policeman. He had also been using a stolen American Express credit card to lavishly entertain two girls. Further prison sentences also followed. He was introduced to Fiona while he was labouring in Deptford on the Pepys Estate. From labouring, he had boldly set himself up in fashionable Regent Street as a financial adviser. When his advice was no longer sought, he turned to driving a van for a living, which was his last job before becoming employed by the Cleavers, and moving, with his wife, into the servants' quarters, a two-bedroomed cottage in the grounds. They had been there only a fortnight when Joseph Cleaver was shocked by Fiona's black eye.

A few nights later, Fiona fled for her life and slept under the bed of the Cleavers' nurse, making her final escape the next morning. George Stephenson was fired that same morning of August 7, 1986.

After Fiona's visit to Scotland Yard, a photograph of Stephenson was circulated to the media. Early the next morning, Hampshire detectives raided a house in Bournemouth, where they found a television set which had belonged to the Cleavers. Now they knew the trail was hotting up. From that address, they learned that Stephenson was driving a 'C' registration Rover car. The next day, Hampshire police received information from Parkside Motors, Coventry, that one of their hire cars, a red Rover, registration C352 YRW, had been rented on the Monday to three men. The vehicle had been returned on the Tuesday, the bill being paid by cheque by a George Daly.

On the Wednesday evening, George Stephenson gave himself up to police in the New Forest at the Roundhill camp site. He had caught a train from Coventry, devoting the evening to drinking and flirting in Brockenhurst. George Daly, Stephenson's friend, was arrested by thirty armed officers at 2 a.m. in Coventry on Thursday. Daly's brother, John, was detained later that same morning as he walked along a Coventry street.

As the investigation continued, the detectives learned that the rubber gloves the gang wore during the killings had been bought at Boots Chemist in central Bournemouth. The twine they used to bind their victims had come from a hardware shop in Westbourne, a cosmopolitan area on Bournemouth's western boundary with Poole. The stockings for the masks had been bought in the Bournemouth branch of Debenhams.

At the trial at Winchester Crown Court, George Stephenson was given six life sentences with a recommendation from the judge, Mr Justice Hobhouse, that he should serve a minimum of twenty-five years. The judge told him: 'These murders were committed in circumstances of indescribable brutality and cruelty. You were the leader. You showed no mercy and deserve none.' John Daly, aged twenty-one, received seven life sentences for rape, robbery, burning alive the four captives and strangling Wendy Cleaver. Twenty-five-year-old George Daly was acquitted of murder but was convicted of manslaughter. The judge said that the jury were not sure that he had 'intended to kill,' but that he had displayed 'a reckless disregard for human life'.

During the trial, it was alleged that George Stephenson had decreed it essential that all three of them should rape Wendy Cleaver.

It was also revealed that Tom Cleaver had £700-worth of British and United States currency on him, plus a batch of travellers cheques, which the killers failed to find because he had hidden them in his artificial limb. Neither did the gang manage to locate the wall-safe, which was concealed in the master bedroom, where most of the slaying took place. In the end, they had to settle for a paltry £90, which worked out at £18 a life; a very mean rate of exchange.

From the outside, Burgate House has changed very little. Fordingbridge continues to mourn. Some might say that a way of life, and a certain style, died with the massacred Cleavers: I would be the first to agree with them.

6

□□■□□

Deadman's Hill

■ WHEN I was employed as a crime correspondent with the now defunct *Daily Herald*, I used to commute between Bedford and London. Occasionally, I made the hundred-mile return journey by car. It was not a particularly scenic drive, except for a three-mile stretch of the A6 approximately halfway between the village of Elstow, John Bunyan's birthplace, and Luton.

Driving south, the road is as meandering as the nearby River Ouse. Suddenly and unexpectedly, it straightens out and rises steeply. There is a farm on the left-hand side and the monotonous, predictable hedged fields begin to be gobbled up by pine forests. When you know every quirk and wart of a road, you tend to follow it blindfold, but that would be impossible on this section of the undulating A6: particularly since August 23, 1961.

At the crown of the incline, the road forks into dual carriageway. On the right, assuming you are heading towards London, is a lay-by; one of the largest of its kind. Not only is it very long, but the arc of its horseshoe curve is deep, curling inland a considerable distance from the main road. It is a perfect spot for picnickers and lovers because it is totally eclipsed from the busy A6 by a screen of bushes. Somebody with morbid prescience had named that part of the road 'Deadman's Hill', originating from the days of highwaymen and the gibbets, which were erected to despatch them.

Of course, when Michael Gregsten, a talented research

scientist, drove into the Deadman's Hill lay-by in the early hours of the morning of August 23, 1961, he was approaching from the opposite direction, travelling north towards Bedford, and heading for an unknown final destination. Beside him, in the front passenger seat, was his lover, Valerie Storie. Their self-imposed passenger was in the rear seat, holding a gun to the back of Gregsten's head.

Summer was in full spate; the previous day had been a scorcher and as a result it was now stifling. There was not a single cloud, and it was typical of many similar nights I have witnessed on Deadman's Hill. I once stopped there during my courting days. We were not alone; a convoy of parked cars was evidence of a plagiarized idea. We cursed the moon; it was so bright that we might as well have been sitting in a living room with all the lights on. Spidery figures in the other vehicles weaved their own web of involvement. Headlights from the distant road probed the darkness, lingering like a Peeping Tom's torch. It seems so long ago.

Unfortunately for Gregsten and Miss Storie, the Deadman's Hill lay-by was a lonely, desolate killer's lair by the time they chanced upon it. But let us turn back the clock a few hours...

Gregsten, who was separated from his wife, had gone for a drink at a pub in Taplow, near Slough in Berkshire, with Miss Storie, a work colleague with whom he was having a serious affair. The quaint pub on the banks of the River Thames was an ancient inn-type watering-hole, redolent of ye olde worlde charm and atmosphere. It was not the first time they had been there. In summer time, it was something of a lovers' honeypot, especially on sultry nights when the garden bar was open.

Michael and Valerie did not have a great amount to drink on the evening of August 22. They sat on the bench seats at a table close to the river's edge, the romantic setting inspiring thoughts and talk. Michael and Valerie had neither eyes nor ears for anything or anyone other than themselves. They were absorbed in intimacy. The conversation was fast, the drinking slow. They were earnestly making plans for a future together which they did not have. Their parting that night was to be a final separation.

From the pub they drove to a beauty spot known as Dorney Reach, where they sat talking peacefully, blissfully, in the way that lovers do. They had been there about half-an-hour when someone tapped on the driver's window. Gregsten probably thought that the face against the glass belonged to a policeman or farmer. Certainly he experienced no premonition of danger. With a sigh, he wound down his window, while Miss Storie looked on curiously. Before he had time to grasp what was happening, he was staring into the menacing open mouth of a revolver.

'Gimme the ignition keys,' the man demanded. Naturally, Gregsten did as he was ordered.

As soon as the keys had been handed over, the gunman climbed into the back seat, immediately launching into a rambling monologue about himself, complaining, most of the time, about the unfairness of life. As a youth, he said, he had been reared without love in Borstal and remand homes. The implication of his soliloquy was that he had drawn life's short straw. For something like two hours he droned on to his truly captive audience.

As far as Miss Storie could recall, it must have been around midnight when the gunman started to become agitated, deciding that Gregsten should be incarcerated in the boot.

Gregsten was stunned by the command and would have tacitly complied but for the strenuous protest on his behalf by Miss Storie. She begged the gunman not to lock up her lover, warning of the dangers of suffocation and carbon-monoxide poisoning. Reluctantly, he relented, deciding instead that they should go for a drive. 'Head for London Airport,' he told Gregsten, returning the ignition keys.

Naturally, the couple believed that their hijacker intended fleeing the country by air. He had already let it be known that he was 'on the run' from police forces all over the country. The gun was pressed into Gregsten's neck as they headed unhurriedly towards Heathrow. The gunman left Gregsten in no doubt what would happen to him if he did anything to try to attract police attention.

While Miss Storie sat in stony silence, though still optimistic about the outcome, their uninvited passenger continued to regale them with his own stories of misfortune. He said he was desperate for a cigarette, but neither Gregsten nor Miss Storie smoked. Unable to resist his craving, he made Gregsten pull up beside a cigarette machine. 'Get me a packet,' he demanded. When asked what brand, he replied: 'Any. You choose.'

Before Gregsten left the car, the gunman reminded him what would happen to Miss Storie if he did 'anything silly'. Now the pistol was pointing at the head of Gregsten's lover.

The journey to nowhere-in-particular continued, with the gunman chain-smoking. The couple looked at one another as they were directed away from the airport, travelling across country in a detour of London until they were motoring north on the A6. St Albans and Luton were soon behind them. Traffic was spasmodic: not once did they encounter a police car. The gunman, becoming increasingly edgy by the minute, kept his eyes on the dashboard. Gregsten wisely ensured that he did not exceed the speed limit. The revolver was always lowered whenever a vehicle either approached or came up behind.

They must have been driving for at least a couple of hours and the hijacker was showing signs of weariness, continually yawning as he tried to keep himself awake with a non-stop flow of chatter.

A village disappeared as quickly as it had appeared. The brief glimpse they had convinced them that the world was sound asleep. The dual carriageway caught them by surprise. The scenery had changed quite suddenly. Wide open spaces, prairie-like acres, had been replaced by hills and woodland. Long curves first took the road in a prolonged sweep to the right, and then in a similar manner to the left. The lights of the village High Street had retreated into oblivion. A summer breeze, like hot breath, kept the trees gently on the move.

Traffic, like glow-worms, had gone to ground. None of them knew that they were on Deadman's Hill.

The headlights illuminated the blue-and-white lay-by sign. They were almost upon the entrance when the gunman made up his mind. 'In there!' he ordered, indicating the lay-by. Gregsten had to brake sharply and swerve. When they were at the furthest point from the main road, Gregsten was told to stop the car and switch off the engine, which he did. Gregsten and Miss Storie must have been wondering: 'What now?'

They did not have to wait long for an answer. The gunman intimated that he planned to rest, telling them: 'I want to kip.' First, though, he would have to tie them up. But what did he intend doing with them finally, they wanted to know. That, he said, he would have to 'fink about'.

A length of rope was used to tie Miss Storie's wrists. Then it was Gregsten's turn. The gunman was anxious to secure Gregsten to his seat. 'Give me that bag up,' he said to the driver. He was pointing to a laundry bag beside Miss Storie's feet.

As Gregsten turned sideways and leaned forwards, two shots were fired in quick succession, both of them hitting the talented research scientist in the head, killing him instantly.

Miss Storie screamed: 'You shot him, you bastard! Why did you do that?'

The killer replied: 'He frightened me. He moved too quick. I got frightened.'

The distraught laboratory assistant implored the gunman to allow her to drive Gregsten to the nearest hospital, but all he would say was: 'Be quiet, will you, I'm finking.' Those words were to provide the noose around his neck.

Just a few seconds later, he was to repeat the word 'finking', which Miss Storie would never forget — not for the rest of her life.

When Miss Storie was ordered into the back of the car, she refused, fully realizing what he had in mind. It was then made clear that if she did not remove her knickers and join the murderer on the back seat, she, too, would be shot. Miss Storie did not need any convincing that her captor was capable of cold-blooded extermination.

Tearfully, Miss Storie did as she was told, her hands having been untied after the murder. Her attacker watched every move as she wriggled out of her underwear, leaving her panties on the front seat as she squeezed into the rear.

While her murdered lover remained in the driver's seat, Miss Storie was raped in the back of the car in a clumsy, feverish frenzy, the gun held to the temple of her head. Then she was forced to help drag Gregsten's body from the car on to the grass. That done, Miss Storie found herself having to teach her rapist and subsequent killer how to drive the car. He demanded to be shown how to start the engine, and the configuration of the gears.

Emotionally overcome, Miss Storie flopped to the ground, sobbing uncontrollably, and that is when she, too, was shot — five times. One bullet thudded into her neck; the other four penetrated her shoulder and arm. The moment she was hit by the first shot, she lost sensation in her legs. From that moment, she was paralysed from the waist downwards and has never walked since. Apparently satisfied that she was dead, the murderer climbed back into the car and drove away.

Miss Storie, unable to move and convinced that she would die before being found, was still semi-conscious at 6.30 a.m. when she and Gregsten were discovered by a farm labourer.

Scotland Yard's Detective Superintendent Bob Acott led the murder hunt. The Home Office pathologist whom Acott called for was Professor Keith Simpson, who joined the detectives at the scene of the crimes. From Deadman's Hill, he went to Bedford General Hospital, where Miss Storie was in intensive care and Gregsten was in the mortuary.

The Professor wasted no time starting the autopsy. Taking into account rigor mortis and temperature factors, he was able to establish the time of death between three and four o'clock that morning. Later, he was to tell Acott that Gregsten had been shot from a range of no more than two inches. The bullets had gone completely through his head, from the left ear to his right cheek. A 0.32 calibre handgun had been the weapon.

A few days later, Professor Simpson returned to Bedford General Hospital to examine Miss Storie, and he was able to report that she had been shot by the same gun that had been used on Gregsten; and that one of the bullets had become lodged in her spine, causing permanent damage. This may seem obvious but was nonetheless a necessary formality as the police pieced together the intricate jigsaw.

Then the investigation moved along at a whirlwind tempo. The car had been abandoned in Ilford, Essex, and the murder weapon had been hidden under the seat of a London bus. Acott was sure that the killer was 'holed-up' in the capital, possibly being shielded by a girlfriend, wife or mother, so he made several appeals to the public and was soon reaping his reward.

A male landlord in Finsbury Park, north London, telephoned to say that he had a 'suspicious character' living in his house who had rented a room the day after the murder, and had not emerged since. This was the kind of breakthrough for which Acott had been praying.

The man Acott and his men escorted from that address was Peter Louis Alphon, although he was using the name Durrant. A quick check of his background revealed that he was the son of a clerk in the criminal records department at Scotland Yard!

Alphon earned a living as a door-to-door salesman, selling almanacs. When questioned about the murder and rape, he said that on the night of August 22 he had stayed at the Vienna Hotel in Maida Vale, north-west London, once again using the name Durrant. The police checked out his alibi and it tallied; he had, indeed, stayed at the Vienna Hotel — in Room 6. With that confirmed, Alphon was released.

At the end of the first week in September, a housewife in Richmond advertised that she had a room to let. The first caller in response to that advertisement tried to rape her the moment they reached the bedroom, tying her hands, pushing her on to the bed, raising her dress and declaring: 'I'm the A6 murderer, so you'd better shut up and do as you're told.' Her response was to scream her head off, and he fled.

The trail went cold for a couple of weeks, until the 24th, when the manageress of the Vienna Hotel was cleaning Room 24. As she moved an armchair, something fell on to the carpet. She knelt down and picked up a spent cartridge. Looking to see where it had come from, she discovered a hole in the side of the chair. When she pushed her hand into the rent, she pulled out a second cartridge.

The same day, detective scientists were able to prove that the cartridges found in the Vienna Hotel had come from the gun that was used to kill Gregsten. However, the man who had spent the night of the murder in Room 24 had signed the register J. Ryan. Nevertheless, Acott wasted no time in declaring publicly that Peter Alphon was a suspect — especially after interviewing the former manager of the Vienna Hotel, who had been on duty on the night of August 22, although he was no longer employed there.

The former manager had told Acott that on August 22/23 he had gone to bed at 2 a.m. and Alphon (Durrant) had still not returned.

Acott could not believe his luck on September 22 when Alphon telephoned and made an appointment to give himself up. During that first interview, Alphon maintained that on the night in question, he had been visiting his mother in Streatham in south London. Mrs Alphon was approached and she failed to corroborate her son's alibi. Alphon insisted that he had returned to the Vienna Hotel at 11 p.m. The manager that night, a Mr Nudds, was adamant that Alphon was lying.

The next morning, Acott arranged an identification parade. The woman who had almost been raped when she showed upstairs a caller to her house, ostensibly looking for accommodation, missed Alphon in the line up, only to collapse afterwards and declare that he *was* the man. By then, of course, it was too late. Mr Nudds paused at Alphon and said that he 'could be' the Mr Durrant who had occupied Room 6. Two other witnesses walked down the line without stopping once. From the point of view of the police the identification parade had been a disaster.

Everything was to hinge on the main witness who, of course, was Miss Storie. By that time, she had been transferred to Guy's Hospital in London where, by chance, Professor Simpson was based. Acott was refused permission to see Miss Storie that day because she was in the operating theatre, having two bullets extracted by Dr Rennie.

Acott was finding it increasingly difficult to justify keeping Alphon in custody, so it was only natural that he pressed Dr Rennie for an identification parade to be set up in the hospital. A formula was agreed for the 24th. Twelve men, one of them the suspect, were paraded in a corridor. Miss Storie was wheeled in her bed from the ward and passed the line up. Then she was pushed along the corridor in the opposite direction, giving her plenty of time to recognize the man who had been with her all those hours in the car, finally murdering her lover, raping her and then permanently paralysing her. She pointed to an innocent Spanish sailor! Alphon walked free and Acott and his team had to begin all over again, although not entirely from scratch.

The new prime suspect became the James Ryan who had stayed in Room 24 at the Vienna Hotel, where the cartridges had been found. A couple of days later, one of Acott's men received a tip from an underworld informant that there was a petty crook called James Ryan (although his real name was James Hanratty) aged twenty-five, who had a police record for crimes of burglary and stealing cars. Once again, Acott involved the press in his manhunt and wasted no time circulating details of Hanratty, including a Rogues' Gallery 'mug shot'.

Suspect number one, Alphon, had contacted Acott, and now it was Hanratty who followed suit. In a telephone conversation, which the police did not have time to trace, he explained that he had been in Liverpool with three villains on the night of the murder, but he was not prepared to come forward because he was wanted for housebreaking.

The police dragnet was intensified and every officer in the United Kingdom was looking for Hanratty. Although no complete trace had been possible on his call, they had pinpointed it to the north-west. Liverpool became the eye of the storm, so to speak, in view of Hanratty's claim to having been there on August 22 and 23, and the police were not far off target. On October 11, two uniformed policemen in Blackpool, just forty-seven miles north of Liverpool, detained a man they believed to be Hanratty. The hunt was over.

Another identification parade was hurriedly assembled after Hanratty had been collected by Acott and driven south. This time every one of the twelve men was asked to say: 'Be quiet, I'm thinking.' The moment Hanratty spoke, Miss Storie said: 'That's him!' He had pronounced this 'finking'.

Hanratty was hanged at Bedford Prison on April 4, 1962, but in many ways it was the start of the case rather than its conclusion. Not long after Hanratty's execution, Alphon began making a series of confessions that he was the A6 murderer and rapist. The journalist and author, Paul Foot, believed him and wrote a book to that effect in collaboration with Alphon. On the other side of the argument is Professor Simpson, who is satisfied that there has been no miscarriage of justice.

Paul Foot and two other authors — Louis Blom Cooper and Lord Russell of Liverpool — could not believe that an experienced car thief, which Hanratty was, would need to be shown how to start a car and to change the gears. However, Professor Simpson was swayed by Miss Storie's testimony and that of two other prosecution witnesses. In his own book, he wrote: 'I myself do not doubt that the Crown case has in no way been seriously dented by the books and articles written on the case.'

But this is a book about places rather than about people and post-mortems.

Every night, especially in summer, there is a steady flow of traffic turning into the lay-by on Deadman's Hill. Most of the motorists, of course, know nothing of its gruesome history. It is simply a convenient place to break a long journey, to have a cigarette and a drink from a flask, or to do the things that have always been done by lovers in parked cars.

One couple who will never forget Deadman's Hill lay-by are Sonia and John Darby, from York. They had been on holiday in Devon and Cornwall, when late at night they decided to suspend their drive home. Since mid-day they had been taking it in turns to drive and by midnight they were both very tired. 'We'll look for somewhere to stop for the night,' said John. Within ten minutes they had come across a 'perfect' lay-by at the summit of a hill. All they were aware of at the time was that it was a place somewhere between Luton and Bedford, and still a long way from home!

They were towing a medium-sized caravan into which they climbed within a couple of minutes of stopping. Sleep came easily, but after about three hours John was woken by the headlights of a car passing the caravan. Having been disturbed, he now found that he was unable to get back to sleep.

'I fancied a cigarette, but then realized I'd left the packet in the car,' he recalled. So he slipped into a pair of trousers and old shoes, and went out of the caravan. The other car was parked about ten yards ahead, all of its lights now switched off.

'Something attracted me to that vehicle,' said John. 'I can't explain why, but I was drawn to it, almost against my own will, you might say. I couldn't see anyone in the car, but there's nothing unusual about that. I mean, the driver could have gone for a leak or there might have been a courting couple lying low on the back seat. I was not snooping: I had no more control over myself than a piece of metal that has got too close to a magnet.'

The driver's window had been wound halfway down. So, too, had been the passenger window behind the driver, from which cigarette smoke wafted. John, who had a flashlight with him, was astonished when the car still appeared to be empty. By now, he was alongside the vehicle, brushing against a rear door, its interior floodlit by his torch.

And that was the moment when he heard the words from the

back seat: 'Be quiet, I'm finking.' Yet there was no one there. He put his head through the half-open back window; still cigarette smoke curled upwards, and a disembodied voice repeated: 'Be quiet, I'm finking.'

Mystified, John hurried to his own car, collected his cigarettes and returned to the caravan, only to discover that he had woken his wife. He told her what had happened and she laughed at him, saying: 'Come on, I'll make a cup of tea.'

As she put on the kettle in the kitchen section of the caravan, which was at the front, she commented: 'I thought you said the car you looked into was parked in front of us?'

'It is,' John replied, joining his wife at the window, only to find that they had the lay-by to themselves. No car could have left in that short space of time without them hearing the engine start and seeing the headlights.

The date was August 23, 1969, the eighth anniversary of the shooting of Michael Gregsten and Valerie Storie, of which John and Sonia Darby were totally ignorant until several years later when relating that experience to a friend, who had been a policeman in the Bedfordshire force.

Deadman's Hill was Miss Storie's hell on earth. Perhaps it is now Hanratty's, too!

7

□□■□□

No. 105, Onslow Gardens

■ SOUTH Kensington Underground Station is busy from morning until night. It is not one of those Tube stations with a pulse geared to the heart-beat of commuters. It is served by the Piccadilly, District and Circle lines, and throbs to the vibration of hurrying feet from morning until the end of evening.

On a bright summer's day, I boarded a Circle Line train at Embankment. It was a few minutes after two thirty in the afternoon and the train had a light load. The doors slid closed without any last-minute passengers squeezing through. Twenty minutes and five stops later, I was being carried on a human wave up the steps towards the ticket hall and exit.

What a difference five stops can make! South Kensington was a floodtide of people. It was pointless trying to go against the flow. The momentum of others carried me beyond the barrier and to the telephones, and that is where I jumped off the conveyor belt.

There were several telephones to choose from. I have no idea if I selected the correct booth. The important point is that the telephones are still there, in exactly the same spot, and the bustling, cosmopolitan character of South Kensington is as prevalent today as it was in 1959. Around the same time on July 13, 1959, the number of one of those telephones was KNI 2355. Of course, the letters were dropped long ago and with more modern equipment came new numbers.

It was from the pay phone KNI 2355 on the afternoon of July 13, 1959, that a call was made to an attractive American fashion model, who lived nearby in fashionable Roland Gardens. Thirty-year-old Mrs Verne Schiffman had been hovering by her telephone, but she did not rush to answer it. Instead, she allowed it to ring at least ten times before picking up the receiver, as directed by Scotland Yard detectives.

Verne had made a complaint to Scotland Yard that a man 'with a guttural accent' had been attempting to blackmail her with 'rigged evidence'. She had nothing to be afraid of and had no intention of giving this 'pest' a penny, but she wanted him off her back because he was becoming a nuisance. The police said she had done the right thing in going straight to them. 'He won't give up,' they predicted. 'He'll press his luck — and we'll be waiting.'

That morning, Mrs Schiffman had been given her final instructions on how to answer the telephone to give the police the best possible chance of tracing the call. 'Talk slowly. Make him repeat everything. If it's local, we won't need very long. If it's out of town, we're talking about minutes, so everything depends on you.'

When the call came, the fashion model carried out her instructions to the letter. The blackmailer was using the name 'Fisher' and the police were listening to every word. Mrs Schiffman exploited all her charm to keep 'Mr Fisher' on the line for several minutes — long enough for the telephone engineers to trace the call.

'It's local,' a detective was informed at Chelsea Police Station. 'Knightsbridge 2355, a public phone at South Kensington Underground Station.' The Tube station was just a couple of blocks from Roland Gardens, where the model lived, and a five-minute car dash from Chelsea Police Station. The two detective sergeants who were despatched to the Underground station were Raymond Purdy and John Sandford.

The entrance to the station was obstructed by people, some browsing at the bookstall, others queuing for tickets, or waiting for someone, or for a booth to become vacant. Women wore summer frocks. Businessmen carried their jackets over their arms, shirt collar-buttons undone and neckties loosened. London was in the grip of a heat-wave, which was reflected in the pace of city life. Everything had become discernibly slower. People in a hurry walked. This did not apply, though, to detectives Purdy and Sandford. They parked their car half on the pavement and sprinted towards the bank of pay phones.

All the telephone kiosks were occupied, so they had no alternative but to pull open the doors and check the number on the dials. It was second time lucky for them. 'Okay, lad, we're police officers,' Purdy said to the man who was still talking with Mrs Schiffman.

Sandford took hold of the receiver and spoke with the model, telling her: 'We've got him. Thanks for your co-operation. Well done. There's nothing for you to worry about any more.'

The suspect was pulled from the telephone box and made to put his arms behind his back ready for handcuffing. At that moment, he lashed out with his feet, elbowed Purdy in the stomach, pushing him into Sandford, and fled, scattering the crowds.

Quickly the detectives picked themselves up and ran after their man, bringing traffic to a standstill as they sped into the road without regard for their own safety.

South Kensington has always been one of London's most fashionable addresses. Today it has lost some of its esteem. The Old Brompton Road has become a labyrinth of bed-sitters, a spillover from nearby Earl's Court. But the big houses still stand, and resting unobtrusively within sight and sound of the tumultuous main roads are the stately squares and the occasional mews, as dignified as ever.

It was to one of these grand squares that the fleeing blackmailer headed. He chased breathlessly around Onslow Square, cutting into Onslow Gardens, where he ducked into No. 105, a majestic old residence that had been converted into apartments. The imposing entrance was typical of its type — wide, well-scrubbed steps, Roman-styled pillars and beefy black doors, brass-studded and bearing numerous nameplates.

The chase seemed to be all over when an arrest was made in the cool entrance hall. The prisoner, held firmly by Purdy, sat on the window-ledge, getting his breath back, while Sandford went in search of the housekeeper — though she was not in her room.

'You'll be sorry for giving us the run-around,' Purdy predicted, once again preparing to clip on the handcuffs. Just at that moment, Purdy turned his head towards Sandford, probably because the other detective was not having any luck in his efforts to raise the housekeeper. For Purdy, it was to prove a deadly lapse of concentration. In the brief second that he took his eye off the prisoner, he was shot dead.

Why the prisoner was not searched immediately remains a mystery: and why was there such a delay before Purdy thought to handcuff the prisoner? The answers, of course, died with Purdy.

Sandford went to the aid of his colleague, hoping that he was still alive, during which time the prisoner made his second escape.

Now the blackmail attempt was of little consequence. The case had escalated into a murder hunt. A policeman had been gunned-down in cold blood. No policeman in the land, whatever his rank, would rest until the murderer was in custody. 'Suddenly this has become very personal,' one senior Scotland Yard officer was quoted as saying. 'I'm not suggesting for one minute that we try any less in other murder investigations, but when a fellow police officer is killed, well, it's family. We're only human, just like anybody else.'

Purdy had taken a small notebook from the killer's pocket during the first arrest at the Underground station. This was now examined by Murder Squad detectives and proved most revealing. Listed were a number of flats in Roland House, Roland Gardens, all of which had been burgled during the past few days. One of the apartments broken into at Roland House was the residence of Mrs Schiffman. In addition to taking some money and jewels, the burglar had stolen documents which, mistakenly, he had thought would incriminate the owner. It was because she had nothing whatsoever to fear that Mrs Schiffman had immediately contacted the police. Also in the notebook were a number of names, addresses and telephone numbers — contacts of the killer.

Forensic detectives wasted no time investigating the window-ledge where the killer had been sitting just before shooting Purdy. They were lucky: a full recent thumb print had been left on the window. If the killer was a professional burglar and/or blackmailer, there was every chance that he had a criminal record. Interpol was also alerted in case he should try to escape to Europe, especially in view of his accent, which had suggested that he was not British.

Every person in that notebook was contacted within a few hours of the killing and within twenty-four hours Scotland Yard had the name of the cop killer: Guenther Fritz, Podola, aged thirty — a German who had been living in Canada, from where he had been deported because of his criminal activities. From Canada, he had flown to Düsseldorf, only to fall foul of the West German police. In May, 1959, he had arrived in Britain, making straight for London and embarking on an orgy of crime in the upper-class playgrounds of the West End.

A photograph of Podola appeared on the front page of every national newspaper and an extra vigil was kept on all air and sea ports.

On the day of the murder, a man signing the register as Paul Camay had checked into the Claremont House Hotel at No. 95, Queen's Gate, Kensington, about half-a-mile from Chelsea Police Station. He had been given Room 15, but he never went out. It was a small, unpretentious establishment without a restaurant, and Mr Camay always sent the owner to fetch him a sandwich and a beer, finally arousing suspicion, especially as he bore a striking resemblance to the wanted police killer.

And so it was that on Thursday, July 16, a call was made from the proprietor of the Claremont House Hotel to Chelsea Police Station. 'All he does is lay on his bed smoking and listening to his portable radio,' the police were told. 'He sends me out to buy his cigarettes and food.'

The police checked on the date and time of his arrival at the Hotel. Within fifteen minutes, they had the whole of Queen's Gate cordoned off. This time there would be no mistake: no one was going to slip through this net. The three plainclothes officers who mounted the stairs to Room 15 were Inspector Vibart, Sergeant Chambers and Detective Morrissey, two of them with dogs.

The owner was asked if he would be prepared to help and he obliged willingly. 'Tap on the door,' he was told, 'and say you've brought him some cigarettes.'

'I've never done that before,' said the owner. 'He always asks me first and gives me the money. Won't he think it's a bit odd?'

'It's worth a try.'

But there was no answer, even after three or four knocks on the door.

'Okay, you go downstairs and leave this to us,' the owner was told.

Sergeant Chambers, who weighed more than 16 stone, pushed ahead of the Inspector, promising: 'I'll have this door down in one go!' And then, rapping on the door sharply, he called out: 'Police! Open up!' But the only response was a clicking noise, like the sound of a gun being cocked.

Bracing himself, Chambers promptly used his body as a battering ram. True to his word, the door yielded on the first charge. In went the dogs, followed by Chambers and the other two detectives. The door and Chambers landed on Podola, whose gun was under his pillow. In the ensuing struggle with the officers and the dogs, Podola landed in the fireplace, with his head almost up the chimney. As he was led from the hotel, Podola was sporting a massive black eye.

At Chelsea Police Station, Podola was charged with the murder of Detective Sergeant Purdy and then went into shivering and twitching spasms, finally becoming unconscious, whereupon he was admitted to the nearby St Stephen's Hospital in Fulham. However, on the 20th, doctors considered him fit enough to be taken to West London Magistrates'

Court, where he was formerly remanded in custody to Brixton Prison to await trial at the Old Bailey.

The trial began on September 10, with defence counsel, Mr Frederick Lawton, QC, claiming that Podola was suffering from amnesia as a result of injuries incurred during his arrest. Four doctors gave evidence for the defence, including the neurologist, Dr Colin Edwards, who had examined Podola on July 21 and September 10. The two prosecution doctors, however, were convinced that Podola was malingering. The first question the jury had to answer was whether or not Podola was fit to face trial for murder. After eleven days of submissions, the jury retired for three hours and decided the defendant's loss of memory was faked.

Consequently, a new jury was sworn in and a fresh trial began three days later, this time to judge nothing other than the facts relating to the shooting of Purdy. Podola pleaded not guilty and was defended once again by Mr Frederick Lawton. Prosecuting was Mr Maxwell Turner, the Recorder of Hastings and the senior Treasury Counsel at the Central Criminal Court.

Three days later, Podola was found guilty and sentenced to death. He was hanged on November 5.

Today, no one on the run would find refuge in the hallway of No. 105, Onslow Gardens. Although it remains a house of apartments, the front door is kept locked, and no one can wander in without a key. In the last thirty years, security has become a much greater problem. The hall has been smartened up considerably since the end of the Fifties, but somehow today's echoes seem to evoke the past: the striking of a high heel on marble could almost be mistaken for the crack of gunfire. The window is clean and the ledge spotless; the pillars are polished daily. However, no amount of purging of the past will ease a widow's mourning, and a child's grief for the loss of his father. Buildings may even be knocked down, but the events of the past cannot be eradicated.

8

□□■□□

The Blind Beggar

■ *THE Blind Beggar* in the East End of London has always had the reputation of being a man's pub. Spit and sawdust, heady ale, strong language, blue jokes and red politics. A working man's refuge; not the sort of place to impress a new girlfriend or even an old wife. An image, however, that a facelift has successfully wiped away.

As long ago as the 1890s, *The Blind Beggar*, poised pugnaciously between Whitechapel Underground Station and Cambridge Heath Road, symbolized the hard-nosed image of gangland. In fact, one of the most notorious bunch of mobsters ever spawned in the cockney East End was named after *The Blind Beggar* pub, which became the headquarters where they plotted their forays into the ritzy West End and the race-tracks to thieve and mug. They were proud of their infamy, boasting that they had killed a man at the bar, thrusting a metal umbrella-tip through his eye and into his brain; this was for no less than his refusal to leave the pub when ordered out by 'The Blind Beggar Gang', who wanted to be alone to plan their next crime-wave. It is an apocryphal story, with only a meagre element of truth, but the lie has flowered over the years.

Unfortunately, there was nothing exaggerated about the sadistic brags of The Blind Beggar Gang's successors, the Kray Twins. No one who lived through the 1950s and 60s will ever forget their reign of terror. For acts of gratuitous violence, they had no equal except, perhaps, for the Richardson Brothers whose evil thugs controlled all London territory south of the river. The Krays dominated the east and west and neither mob had been stupid enough to breach the demarcation line. However, George Cornell, the chief architect of the Richardson Brother's criminal expertise, was not renowned for his diplomacy, and had won no friends among the East End gang barons by making public jokes about Ronnie Kray's homosexual proclivities. Ronnie Kray was further enraged when the father of his live-in boyfriend was contacted by George Cornell who enlightened him about his son's 'affair'.

All the more surprising, therefore, that Cornell should have 'trespassed' on the evening of March 8, 1966, taking himself for a drink in the lion's den, *The Blind Beggar*.

The Blind Beggar was the sort of pub that went through an early evening lull. At eight o'clock on March 8, there were only five customers, including Cornell, in the bar drinking light ales, plus a barmaid. One of them made a whispered telephone call to another pub, *The Lion*, just half a mile away in Tapp Street, where Ronnie Kray was drinking with one of his most feared and trusted henchmen, John Barrie.

At 8.30 exactly, two of the men in the bar at *The Blind Beggar* finished their drinks and said they had to leave on 'urgent business'. The other three continued drinking, but only for about five minutes. The door flew open and in strutted Ronnie Kray, flanked by Barrie. The scene was something straight out of a Wild West saloon showdown.

Cornell turned on his stool. On seeing Ronnie Kray, he sneered: 'Well, look who's here!' These were his last words. Kray pulled out a revolver and shot Cornell just above the right eye. Barrie, also producing a pistol, began blasting away at the ceiling, just as a warning. The barmaid had wisely dived for cover behind the bar. Then swaggering in the manner in which they had arrived, Kray and Barrie departed.

Cornell was still alive, but only just. He was taken to the nearby London Hospital, then transferred to the West End Hospital for emergency brain surgery, but all attempts to save his life failed. The post-mortem was performed at the Westminster Mortuary by Professor Keith Simpson.

Detective Superintendent Butler, of Scotland Yard, headed the investigation. Butler had made his name by solving the Great Train Robbers' case. There were three witnesses to the assassination — two customers and the barmaid — yet not one of them could give a description of the killer. Had the gunmen been wearing masks? No. The fear was tangible: the 'I saw nothing, guv' response from witnesses to crimes committed by the Krays was what the police had come to expect.

Despite the reluctance of eye-witnesses to talk, the police knew, almost at once, that this was a gangland execution. Butler's underworld informants soon put him in the picture, and on the third day after the killing, he visited the Kray Twins — Ronnie and Reggie — at their council flat in Lea Bridge Road, Walthamstow. Both men were 'invited' to Commercial Street Police Station. 'Any time,' quipped Ronnie. 'I hear you brew the best tea in town there!'

The Kray's flat was searched, but no gun was found. Ronnie Kray was put in an identification parade line-up, but the barmaid from *The Blind Beggar* pub walked past the twelve men to declare: 'He's not here. There's no one I've ever seen before.'

Ronnie Kray had banked on there being little motivation for the police to solve the crime. Known, not only as a torturer, Cornell was also into pornography. Who would miss him? Certainly not decent society, the East End villains had reasoned; Ronnie Kray had done the world a favour. Eighteen months later, the murder remained unsolved, although the case had not been closed.

In October, 1967, a violent London hoodlum, known as 'Jack the Hat' McVitie, went to a party in a basement flat in Stoke Newington, North London. The basement of No. 1, Evering Road, was typical of so many single-girl flats of the time. Every city was inundated with them: one bedroom, a lounge-cum-kitchen, shared bathroom, sparsely furnished, pay-as-you-use gas and electricity, black-and-white television, an unmade bed, a skirt on a chair, stockings and underwear on the frayed carpet beside the bed, a week's newspapers waiting to be thrown out, two days' washing-up in the kitchen sink and everywhere the smell of spilled cooking fat.

McVitie was a verminous, larger-than-life character, who modelled himself on the Chicago gangsters of Al Capone's era. It is hard to understand how he was tolerated for so long by a civilized society, with a government in power that placed such emphasis on law and order. The overwhelming evidence is that London was controlled by the lawless.

'Jack the Hat', named because he was so vain about his bald patch that he would never remove his hat — even in bed until the light was out — hired himself out as a killer. A cash payment of £500 was enough to buy anyone's life. The sight of McVitie, sitting at a table in the Regency Jazz Night Club in Hackney, north London, each arm around a girl and a sawn-off shotgun resting in his lap, was a common spectacle. 'Anyone with a face I don't like, I shoot!' he would shout. He meant what he said, and yet seemed immune to prosecution.

The basement flat had been borrowed by the Kray Twins from a girl that night, October 28, but there was no party; just an orgy of motiveless violence. McVitie arrived at the modest residence believing the flat would be crammed with girls and drink, but there was no party — not the kind McVitie had in mind, at any rate, just a lynching party.

Reggie Kray pressed a revolver against McVitie's head and squeezed the trigger. Nothing happened, except the intended victim broke loose and threw himself at a window, only to be dragged back by five burly hoodlums. The pistol was again held to his head but it was still jammed, and Reggie lost his temper, hurling it across the room.

While McVitie was restrained, Ronnie found a carving-knife and handed it to his twin brother, who promptly stabbed 'Jack the Hat' in the face, the chest and abdomen, and finally through the throat, impaling him to the floor. Ronnie then shook Reggie's hand, saying: 'That makes us level again.' They had a pact that if one committed murder, then the other had to do likewise. McVitie had been chosen for no other reason than to even the score.

The body was wrapped in an eiderdown and driven away in the boot of a car, never to be recovered. The 0.32 pistol and the knife were tossed into the Grand Union Canal in Queensbright Road. It was a year before police frogmen plucked the revolver from the sediment of the murky water. The knife was never found.

The day after this murder, McVitie was reported missing by his girlfriend, but the police didn't take much notice because he had always been a nomad. They assumed he had left one bed for another.

The Krays really believed they were beyond the law. A special squad at Scotland Yard had been established with no wider brief than to bring the Krays to book. In charge of that squad were a pair of the country's most talented policemen, Detective Superintendent Jack Du Rose and Detective Chief Inspector 'Nipper' Read. Although their progress was supposed to be shrouded in secrecy, very little failed to reach the ears of the Krays, who bragged about the number of senior policemen on their payroll. Even so, the Krays saw no reason to curtail their criminal plundering, believing that all witnesses would be too scared to ever testify against them — as had always been the case.

The test came on May 9, 1968, when this crack squad rounded up the Kray Twins, their elder brother, Charles, and fourteen of their roughneck hirelings. It was a gamble, because the case against the Krays was far from complete. The strategy was to do a deal with a number of their associates, persuading them to turn Queen's evidence. For this to be achieved, these associates had to be convinced that they would be beyond the reach of the Krays while they remained in prison on remand. Whenever these targeted men were visited in jail by Chief Inspector Read, he disguised himself as a priest or a doctor from the hospital wing, where most of the statements were taken. One prisoner was carried from his cell on a stretcher when there was nothing wrong with him whatsoever: it was for his own protection in order to avoid the Krays becoming suspicious and putting out contracts from within, which was not beyond them.

Another member of that elite band of officers was Detective Superintendent Mooney, who finally made the barmaid at *The Blind Beggar* accept that she owed the truth to society. At an identification parade in Brixton Prison, she fingered Ronnie Kray as the killer of Cornell, which was no small act of bravery. She was the mother of two small children, which was why she had been afraid of becoming involved in the first place. She had seen what the Krays did to people who crossed them. However, now the tide had turned, and she also identified John Barrie as his accomplice. Next to tell all was John Dickson, who had driven Kray and Barrie to *The Blind Beggar*. Ronnie Hart, a cousin of the Kray Twins, who had witnessed the knifing of McVitie, gave the police a chapter and verse account of everything that took place in the basement flat.

The trial at the Old Bailey was presided over by the much-feared judge, Mr Justice Melford Stevenson. Ronnie Kray was charged with murdering Cornell and McVitie. Reggie Kray was indicted for the murder of McVitie. In all, there were ten men in the dock, the other eight on accessory to murder charges. It was to be thirty-five dramatic days before the jury finally convicted all but one of the defendants. In sentencing the Kray Twins to life imprisonment, the judge recommended that they should serve a minimum of thirty years. Charles Kray was sent down for ten years. John Barrie was put away for life for his contribution to the assassination at *The Blind Beggar*.

When I visited *The Blind Beggar* pub at just after 7.30 p.m., I was the fourth customer of the evening. The three other drinkers, all men, were perched on stools at the bar. Two of them were studying horse-racing form in the evening newspaper. The third man appeared to be engaged in a friendly conspiratorial conversation with the present barmaid — not the one who featured in the trial! Everything stopped with my entry. In the East End, strangers are readily recognized as outsiders.

Without a word between them, I sensed that quickly they

had reached a consensus of opinion that I was harmless. The punters returned to the important matters of life, namely the next day's racing prospects. 'If 'e don't win tomorro', 'e never will,' one of them observed, pointing to the name of a horse.

''E ain't got no jockey,' retorted the other.

'But he will 'ave tommoro', when he runs, stupid!'

The insult passed unnoticed. 'I don't like 'em without jockeys. It can't be fancied.'

''Ow do you make that out?'

'If he was fancied, he'd 'ave a jockey booked well in advance. Stands to reason.'

'Cobblers!'

The cockney eloquence of the debate was riveting.

I sidled up to the silent one. 'It's hard to believe this is where it all happened,' I remarked, trying to be casual.

'Where what happened?' (He should have been a politician.)

'The shooting of Cornell.'

That was the cue for the barmaid to walk away.

'Never heard of him.' He didn't take his eyes off his drink. The other two had suddenly stopped talking about racing, wondering whether they might need to update their assessment of me.

'Cornell was shot dead, at this bar, by Ronnie Kray, at exactly this time of the evening.'

'Ronnie Kray? Never 'eard of 'im either.'

In *The Blind Beggar*, the blind eye had also been turned on the past in a manner that is so typical of the East End.

9

□□■□□

The Magdala Tavern

■ THERE are hundreds of pubs in London like the *Magdala Tavern* at the foot of South Hill Park in fashionable Hampstead. I have used it a couple of times after going for a walk on the Heath at the weekend in summer. Flower baskets hang along the outside of this unspectacular but pleasant Charrington's house. The first-floor windows have flower pots on the ledges, and there were chairs and tables on the pavement. Red-brick was featured above the façade, black-and-green paint below. The bar snacks were nothing special, but certainly adequate. For the area, the *Magdala* was unpretentious and honest. It was exactly what it seemed.

Indeed, I doubt whether I should ever have remembered the *Magdala Tavern* had it not been for that Easter Sunday, April 10, in 1955. Just after 9 p.m., Alan Thompson, an off-duty policeman, was supping a pint of beer at the bar when he noticed a woman's face pressed to the outside of one of the windows. Standing just a few feet from the policeman there was a good-looking young man with a very attractive woman a few years younger than him. They were laughing, joking in a carefree and abandoned fashion. To the casual observer, and most definitely to the jealous onlooker, they might have appeared to be in love.

The handsome young man was David Blakely, a daredevil racing driver who was determined to stay in the fast lane in every aspect of his life. The woman at the window was his jilted lover, Ruth Ellis.

Blakely was staying with friends at No. 29, Tanza Road, which climbed steeply from Parliament Hill to the Heath. They were having a party and had run out of beer. 'I'll go,' he had volunteered, when the call went out for more drink. With him went the nanny of his hosts. They were not having an affair, but not for lack of effort by Blakely who was rapidly building a reputation as a reprobate rake.

The party mood extended beyond No. 29, Tanza Road. As it was a holiday weekend, the air was full of high spirits. However, this mood was not shared by the forlorn creature looking in on other people's happiness. Ruth Ellis, a nightclub hostess, which, in her case, was a euphemism for a hooker, was in love. But the man with whom she was besotted had turned his back on her — and now he was doing it again, as he stood at the bar, placing his order and giggling with the shapely, delicate creature beside him. Ruth was too much in love to be able to let him go. If she could not have him, then no one could. Ruth knew exactly what she was going to do, and what would be the penalty. Death was the price she would have to pay, but this, to Ruth, seemed fair and just. She was a high-principled prostitute.

As Blakely left the *Magdala,* clutching the bottles of beer, he had no inkling his life was nearly over. The noise of the bottles in his hands heralded his death. The last person in the world he expected to encounter was the woman he had spurned.

The execution was fired by passion. Ruth had arrived by taxi and hidden herself behind black railings next to a church, directly opposite the pub. As Blakely emerged from the *Magdala,* Ruth stepped out of the shadows, stopping beneath a pool of yellow light from a street lamp. Still Blakely did not see her. She was 'out of mind', and sight.

'David!' Ruth shouted. It was imperative for Ruth that her ex-lover should die knowing who had terminated his life. Castration was the crime Ruth was committing, although to everyone else it was murder. Blakely stopped in his tracks, next to his car, just about to open the door. By that time, Ruth had taken her pistol from her overcoat pocket. She gripped the weapon with both hands, aiming it unsteadily at the man she loved too much to live without. Black-and-white spectacles, with slightly tinted lenses, had slipped from the bridge of her nose, causing her to squint as she tensed herself for the acts of murder and self-immolation: everything she did that night was short-sighted!

From all the evidence, it appears that Blakely was unaware of the danger he was in. Certainly he made no attempt to run at that moment and eye-witnesses did not recall his uttering a single word.

The first bullet missed Blakely completely and became embedded in the door of the pub: fortunately, no one was entering or leaving at that moment. The second shot also jerked away from its intended target, wounding a shocked passer-by. Now the trajectory to Blakely was blocked by his companion. Ruth had no wish to harm anyone other than David. 'Get out of the way!' she ordered, approaching the two of them in short, mechanical stiletto steps. True to form, Blakely tried to use his friend as a shield, but by now Ruth had him clearly in her sights. Her hand was much steadier now. By the time she emptied the chamber, Blakely had two bullets in his back, one in his thigh and the fourth in his left arm. He was dead, and so was Ruth's emotion.

On hearing the first shot, the off-duty policeman had dashed from the pub. It was all over, though, before he was able to disarm Ruth Ellis. 'Would someone call the police, please,' she murmured vaguely. Her right arm fell limply, the gun almost slipping from her fingers. She seemed totally deflated and enervated, all her sap having been drained in one moment of avenging madness. The policeman took the gun from her, while others desperately tried to revive Blakely.

'Is he dead?' she asked, almost like inquiring of somebody whether it might rain tomorrow. 'I'm glad it's all over.'

Within minutes of her arrival in custody at Hampstead Police Station, she was telling a detective: 'I am guilty. Several people saw me. I want to tell you all about it, but I am rather confused.'

The Ruth Ellis story is a tragic one. In France, it would have been regarded a classic crime of passion. In Britain, no such definition was recognized. Murder was murder. If you were guilty, you hanged. Discretion was no part of the law. It is arguable that the jury which convicted Ruth Ellis never believed she would hang, but the one person who was fiercely determined that she should die with a noose around her neck was Ruth Ellis herself. Despite having a son and a daughter, she believed that she had nothing to live for. Death — even violent, judicial execution — seemed to her the best of all options.

Ruth Ellis married young and had two children, but found herself in the divorce court long before domesticity had begun to pall. 'It was a bad marriage,' she told a friend. 'I married because I was pregnant. I wanted a divorce for the same reason. I think there must be more to life than breeding: I could be wrong.' Ruth kept her son, while her husband had custody of their daughter. Earning a living was the problem. What she lacked in formal training, she compensated for with her personality and a flair for improvisation.

Ruth was an attractive, sharp-featured peroxide blonde, who decided that her looks would have to be her meal ticket for the immediate future. Working the West End nightclubs as an hostess was no problem for her; she looked the part, enjoyed champagne and was the sort of woman men were prepared to lavish money on. The pay was meagre, so she was expected to earn her *real* money by going to bed with the men she entertained. This she did without any reservation, but she was not a typical whore and became very angry if ever people referred to her as a tart. Despite her vocation, she had her own code of morality, which she always observed, however much money was offered as an inducement. Stealing, for example, was something she could never countenance, whatever the pressures upon her. In many respects, honesty was an obsession with her. Indeed, it was because of her integrity and businesslike manner with her work that she was made manageress of The Little Club in Brompton Road, Knightsbridge.

With the job went a flat above the club, and she had enough money to pick and choose who she slept with.

Among the regular clientele was a group of motor-racing drivers and their trendy groupies. Twenty-five-year-old Blakely belonged to that clique. His ambition was to become a professional racing driver, but his self-esteem was considerably in excess of his commitment. He was an habitual drunk, even on the eve of a big race, and while drinking he would become argumentative and belligerent. It was within this category that Blakely most assuredly fell. He was always picking fights with other customers in The Little Club and was having to be rescued by his friends: he was an even worse pugilist than he was a racing driver. Despite all his foibles and imperfections, Ruth Ellis found him irresistible, and he turned to her whenever he wanted something, such as money, a bed for the night and a woman to satisfy his sexual needs. She was a convenience for him, nothing more, but Ruth yearned for a permanent and meaningful relationship.

One man offered Ruth everything she wanted. Although considerably older than her, he was fond of her and not short of money. He took care of the boarding school fees for Ruth's son. Whenever she was penniless after lending her last fiver to Blakely, 'Old Faithful' reimbursed her. The fundamental difference between the two men in her life was that one gave and the other took. In black-and-white terms, one was good and the other was bad.

Blakely's roots were firmly planted in the middle ground of society. While he was playing around with Ruth, back in his own world he already had a fiancée, who met with the approval of his parents. Occasionally he would take Ruth to watch him race, but always she felt an outsider and was never accepted by Blakely's friends, who unkindly regarded her as inferior.

Blakely continued to cause disturbances at the club until finally Ruth lost her job and was evicted from the flat. When Ruth moved in with her much older suitor to Goodwood Court, Devonshire Street, she continued to sleep with Blakely in the same bed she shared with her 'sugar daddy'.

Despite being unable to support Ruth, Blakely behaved jealously, assaulting her, frequently in public, and in private gave her the ultimatum: 'Leave him or I leave you.'

Ruth was so besotted with Blakely that she forsook her safe haven in Devonshire Street and found herself a flat at No. 44, Egerton Gardens. 'Hostessing' was her only means of support, which meant that she was sleeping with clients for money. At best, she was a high-class call girl. 'I have to live,' she told Blakely. 'You can't afford to keep me. If I'm going to keep myself, my son and you, I've no alternative.'

Blakely promptly repaid Ruth by leaving her, aided and abetted by his ex-public schoolboy chums in Hampstead. Now he was back with his fiancée, but also dating other girls he picked up at Hampstead's swinging parties.

Ruth could not believe that anyone would cast aside another human being with such callous disregard. By this time, Blakely was living at No. 29, Tanza Road, Hampstead, with a crowd of middle-class party-lovers, and whenever Ruth telephoned she was told rather haughtily that Blakely was elsewhere. She became obsessed by tracking him down. Consequently, she made her own way to Tanza Road on the Good Friday and stood beside a tree opposite No. 29, listening to the noises of a party wafting from the first floor of the large old house.

During the evening, three people — two men and a girl — tumbled from No. 29 and piled into Blakely's car. Blakely drove. Beside him in the front passenger seat was the woman. It was at that moment Ruth knew that her own life was over — and so was Blakely's. She went home, got herself a gun — no one knows where she obtained it — and returned to Tanza Road on the Sunday, later following Blakely to the Magdala Tavern. The rest is history.

Regulars at the *Magdala* still talk about that fateful holiday weekend all those years ago. A chip in the door remains immortalizing the moment when the shooting began. 'I was here that night,' one elderly man said. 'I'll never forget it. How could I? I'd brought my girlfriend out for a drink: we were married that summer and she died two years ago. Just to think,

I've been through a marriage, raised kids, had grandchildren, and retired from work since 1955. That Easter Sunday seems a lifetime away. It *is* a lifetime!

'When the shooting began, I thought it was a car back-firing. It was all over within a couple of seconds. A man at the door shouted: "Someone's been shot! Call an ambulance." He wasn't talking to anyone in particular and I don't think it registered at first. After a few seconds, I went out like everyone else to have a look. What struck me was the serenity of Ruth Ellis. She was so calm, passive and at peace with herself. When I think back, despite her age, she reminded me of someone on her death-bed who had fulfilled her purpose in life and was ready for the end; almost welcoming it.'

A few weeks earlier, Ruth had suffered a miscarriage. She claimed that Blakely was the father of the child. In reality there was no way of telling whether the baby had been Blakely's or was the result of her 'profession.' At first, Blakely had disowned the child in Ruth's womb, only to mourn it after the miscarriage, blaming Ruth's lifestyle for the natural abortion.

From outside the pub, I peered through a contour window, but could see very little in detail. Then I crossed the road and waited as Ruth had, listening to the merriment.

The door of the pub opened. A man in his late twenties paused on the pavement. Would he go left or right? Neither. Instead, he pulled up his overcoat collar and prepared to cross the road, hurrying towards me. Still he hadn't seen me — just as Blakely had been ignorant of his lurking fate.

I abandoned my cover, startling the stranger. For a moment he was apprehensive.

The church clock struck nine. At that point, I was tempted to shout 'David!'

He could have been only a few feet from where Blakely died. We brushed shoulders. 'Sorry,' I said. 'My fault,' he said. Then he was gone, perhaps to return the following night.

David Blakely had not been so lucky.

No. 195, Melrose Avenue and No. 23, Cranley Gardens

■ COME with me to Muswell Hill in north London. It doesn't take long from the West End — no more than fifteen minutes on the tube from Leicester Square to Highgate. The bus journey takes longer, even outside the rush hours, but is much more pleasant, skirting Regent's Park, creeping up Parliament Hill, weaving through Highgate Village and climbing towards the woods and the golf course, finally reaching the rarified air of the capital where it's safe to breathe — but not always safe to live, particularly during the early 1980s.

Between Highgate Village to the south and to the north, Alexandra Palace and the site of the one-time Ally-Pally Racecourse, is Cranley Gardens. This is London at its sober, 'Sunday Best'. In Victorian times, the upper middle-class residents of Muswell Hill could be observed in their horse-drawn carriages and sartorial finery. The area has always been a bourgeois backbone; an upmarket postcode to have and a snob-value telephone number. Cranley Gardens epitomizes the life of lace curtains and labradors.

Let us move along Cranley Gardens about twelve houses among the odd numbers. We are outside No. 23. It looks respectable enough — a tall, white-and-black fronted residence with a neatly-manicured hedge and a low, rather superfluous fence. The front door is hidden within a glass-structured porch. The windows are fragmented into small squares and there are twelve panes of glass in the front downstairs window, and six in the attic window on the third-floor. The attic is very important, as are the drains.

The drainage is good. However, this was not the case early in February 1983, and the residents were protesting strongly.

Number 23, Cranley Gardens, had been divided into flats, which was rather unusual for this district. Most of the houses were owner-occupied, and at the time, No. 23 was rather letting the side down. It was also shabby, and blocked drains, with the inevitable odour, were provoking trenchant complaints from neighbours.

Detective Chief Inspector Peter Jay walked into this situation on the evening of February 9. Why should a senior detective be concerning himself with a domestic drainage problem? Let us turn back the clock twenty-four hours to the arrival of Michael Cottran, the Dyna-rod man, who had been called out by the owner of the house. Tenants had been complaining of being unable to flush their toilets throughout the weekend. Quickly he diagnosed a 'main drainage problem'. The tenant living on the ground-floor directed Cottran to the manhole which led to the drainage network.

Armed with a high-powered flashlight and his specialist tools, he lowered himself into the system, swiftly locating the blockage. There was no way that he could miss the large slabs of white flesh. 'Don't say anything to anyone,' he told the tenant, then reported his findings to his supervisor, who said he would conduct his own inspection the following morning.

During that night, tenants heard footsteps descending and ascending the stairs. 'I thought someone must be having a party, but I didn't hear any music,' one tenant was to comment later.

When Cottran returned in the morning with his chief, they discovered that the drains apparently had been cleared. However, nothing had been done about the stench and the two men decided to carry out a more thorough inspection, which produced a find that was to send both men scurrying to the surface.

Now you will understand the reason for the presence of Detective Chief Inspector Jay, from Hornsey CID, the following evening. He was leaning against the wall in the hallway when a thirty-seven-year-old civil servant, Dennis Nilsen, returned home to his top-floor flat.

'Mr Nilsen?'

'Yes.'

'I'm Detective Chief Inspector Jay.'

'Oh, yes.'

'Do you mind if we have a chat?'

'No, of course not.'

Nilsen led the way.

Inside the flat were bottles of drink — whisky and beer — modern table and chairs, a plain settee, television set, hi-fi system and a room with a spectacular view.

The bathroom was old-fashioned, with an ill-fitting window and a brown-stained, very deep enamel tub.

The kitchen was a typical bachelor's nightmare, and the bedroom was not much better. Chairs and the hooks behind the door were employed as coat-hangers. There was a sleeping-bag on the floor in one corner, and the bed looked as if it hadn't been made for a week or more. Dirty clothes spilled out of the wardrobe.

Jay said something to the effect that he expected Nilsen was wondering why he was there.

'Not really,' Nilsen replied.

Jay then explained that human flesh and the bones of fingers had been recovered from the drains of the house. When Nilsen made no comment, the detective said straight out: 'Where's the rest of the body, Mr Nilsen?'

Without hesitation or fencing, Nilsen answered: 'It's in there, in two plastic bags.' He was pointing towards the wardrobe and he was telling no lie.

Nilsen was informed that he was being arrested and taken to Hornsey Police Station, and Jay's recollection is that the prisoner was perfectly resigned to his fate.

During the car ride to the police station, Jay wanted to know how many victims there were: 'Are we talking about one body or two?'

'Oh, no, more than that; much more. There have been fifteen or sixteen altogether.' Once again, he was not lying.

Dennis Nilsen, a former policeman and a bespectacled Job Centre employee, was Britain's worst mass killer up to that time, but he couldn't tell a lie. Killing came naturally, but lying did not.

Let us leave Cranley Gardens for a while and travel westwards across north London to Melrose Avenue, just south of Cricklewood, and only three blocks from Chatsworth Road, which is noted for the number of Rolls Royces parked in driveways. Most of the houses in Melrose Avenue — a long, far-reaching road disappearing in a straight line beyond the range of the eye — were built in the 1890s. They are bay-fronted with knee-high walls and modest gardens at the back. Most properties are red-bricked, but some houses have been painted. Number 195 is a case in point. It looked very smart in February 1983, with its virgin white façade, let down slightly by a house next door with a 'For Sale' sign in the rather overgrown restricted frontage.

The interest in No. 195, Melrose Avenue, in February 1983, arose from Nilsen's admission to Jay that he had murdered 'between twelve and thirteen' men at that address, which had been his home before moving to Cranley Gardens. The death-toll at the Muswell Hill address had been three.

There has never been anything extra-special about No. 195, Melrose Avenue. Until the 1960s, it had always been the private residence of one family, handed down through the generations. It offered larger than average rooms and lofty ceilings, typical of its era. 'Built to last', was the epithet of the estate agents when it went on the market. By the time Nilsen came on the scene, in November 1975, it had already been converted into flats. The three rooms on the ground-floor were ideal for his purpose. He wanted somewhere big enough to share with his male companion (who was never his lover), a mongrel bitch called Bleep, and a tom cat, which had been abandoned and befriended by Nilsen. He had a passion for animals, especially strays. There was a gentleness about him which the majority of work-colleagues admired. 'Wouldn't hurt a fly,' was an often-used phrase to describe Nilsen. It was absolutely true; he would never swat a fly, but a human being was different!

Undoubtedly, Nilsen was happier in his Melrose Avenue flat than he had been anywhere else. There was a garden, of which he was in charge. He mowed the lawn, grew flowers and trimmed the hedge. At weekends, he would take Bleep for long walks.

When he watched television or listened to his hi-fi, the cat would sleep in his lap. On summer evenings, at dusk, he would sit in the garden, eating a barbecue supper and drinking lots of beer. This was the happiest period of his life. The home was always kept spotlessly clean, Nilsen and his male flat-mate sharing the chores. Nilsen was the expert cook: once it had been his trade, while serving as a professional soldier. He had joined the army even before he was sixteen, as a junior soldier, and by the time he was nineteen he had transferred to the Catering Corps, making quite a name for himself, and also travelling the world to places like Aden, the Persian Gulf, Cyprus and West Germany.

But military service is not an ideal life for a loner. If you cannot mix easily, you quickly become a target, not always for physical abuse but certainly for derision. Nilsen was capable of looking after himself physically, but he went through his entire army career — some twelve years — as an outsider.

As an army cook he had enjoyed a liberal amount of freedom, and during those twelve years he had developed into a heavy drinker, although he never became violent while under the influence. Alcohol tended to make him more reflective: he would compose poetry, read books about country matters, and attend concerts. All his life he had only one girlfriend. They went together on long walks, sharing an interest in the countryside. On Saturday nights, they would dance, but Nilsen had no idea how to extend the relationship. His girlfriend was attractive and intelligent, and would sit beside him while he recited his favourite poetry, often his own. She desperately yearned for the relationship to become physical but Nilsen had no experience. Finally, she had to take the initiative, which was greatly embarrassing to him.

After much soul-searching and many sleepless nights, Nilsen confronted the fact that he was in love. This made him morose, instead of happy. His emotions were causing him to panic. He wanted his girlfriend to become his wife, and wished to be able to hold her and tell her this, but he was terrified of rejection, which was so familiar to him. However, rather than risk being turned down, he dropped her, breaking her heart. Had he proposed, she would undoubtedly have accepted with delight. Dennis Nilsen would have become a happily married man. Today, perhaps, a proud father. Sixteen strangers would, possibly, still be alive.

In 1972, Nilsen had left the army to join the police; but that lasted only eleven months. He liked being in uniform because it reminded him of military life, but he resented the discipline which had been lacking in the Catering Corps, and found the pettiness irritating.

Rejection was a prominent theme in his life, which began on November 23, 1945, in Fraserburgh, Scotland. His parents were continually feuding. His Norwegian father, Olav Nilsen, frequently went 'missing' on drinking sprees which lasted days, sometimes weeks. When he returned, despairingly hungover, he would lash out at his wife, Betty, and the children.

The marriage lasted seven miserable years, long enough to make an indelible impression on Dennis, although he was only four years old at the time of the divorce. When his mother remarried in 1954, becoming Mrs Betty Scott, a family decision was made which, in essence, was Nilsen's induction into the rejection syndrome. It was decided that for the remainder of his boyhood, he should be raised by his grandparents. Even so, he was immensely happy with his grandfather, Andrew Whyte, who thoroughly spoilt him. Many years later, Nilsen was to write: 'I loved Grandad Whyte more than anybody. He was truly my guardian angel. Nothing was too much trouble for him. He worshipped me and I him. He was my *real* father. I thought he would always be there for me to turn to. It never occurred to me that I might ever have to face life without him. Then he died. Just like that! Without warning. My world fell apart. I was devastated. It seemed that everything I ever loved died or went away. I had pets and they died or got lost. I had no confidence in the future. I was afraid what each new day would bring.'

Because of Nilsen's intense love of his grandfather, he was allowed to see his body in the coffin. 'I wish I hadn't,' he wrote in prison. 'It made me lose all faith. I realized he was gone forever, that he wouldn't be waiting for me, that life ended at death. I was shattered. It seemed so unfair. I wondered what would happen to me. Life without my grandad wasn't life at all.'

A few days later, his two racing pigeons were shot dead. The message he learned was that nothing lasted; hope was futile; the future could not be trusted; optimism was a trick, and the world was a devilish deception. The nature of future events had already been defined.

Nilsen's mother and her second husband were living in Strichen, not too far from Fraserburgh, and he moved in with them, staying until the August of 1961, when he joined the army at the first opportunity. 'I had to get away,' he told an NCO. 'I didn't belong. I've never belonged anywhere, except with my grandfather.'

Most of his contemporaries in the army believed he must have been an only child because he seemed to display all the characteristics, but in fact he had an older brother and a younger sister. On one occasion he was spanked by his mother and sent to bed without supper because he had undressed in front of his brother. Apparently, his mother believed it was sinful and immodest for people of the *same* sex — even brothers and sisters — to see each other's private flesh.

'Flesh was a problem in our family,' Nilsen wrote while on remand. 'There's no way of escaping one's own flesh, but life would have been a lot easier if I didn't have any. Flesh was a constant source of embarrassment for my mother. She taught me to be wary of human flesh, but I still believe it can be beautiful, as long as it is not abused. People can abuse their flesh in such a variety of combinations: by eating too much and over-indulging in so many different ways.' He revealed that he was warned that if he ever caught a glimpse of his sister's naked body, nobody would be able to save him from hell. His hatred of homosexuals seemed to be rooted in this puritanical upbringing.

The most critical event in Nilsen's life was the decision by his friend at No. 195, Melrose Avenue, to leave London for a job in antiques in Devon. They had been together for two years and for Nilsen this separation was intolerable. He had never committed a crime in his life, and continued to commute between Muswell Hill and the Job Centre in Leicester Square. However, he was staying out late at night more and more, drinking excessively in the West End and following in the footsteps of his father.

'There's no way of running from your genes and your past, because they are pulling and you are chasing,' he once said. In addition to everything else, Nilsen was a deep thinker, a 'barrack-room philosopher'. He had the intelligence to be a success at most things. Instead, he chose to succeed at becoming one of Britain's most horrendous failures, which gave him a perverse sense of fulfilment.

Nilsen embarked on the road to hell on a night towards the end of December, 1978, when he was drunk in the Cricklewood Arms pub, *Cricklewood Broadway*. He invited an Irishman back to his Melrose Avenue flat, where the drinking continued throughout the night until both were in a drunken stupor. At some point, Nilsen proposed that his new-found drinking partner should stay so that they could celebrate the New Year together. The proposition was rejected and this seems to have provided the motive for the first murder. While the Irishman slept, Nilsen strangled him with a necktie.

After the murder, he stripped the body and scrubbed it from

head to toe in a ritual cleansing fetish, which was to be repeated after every killing. When the wash was complete, he dried the body and dressed it: flesh had not only to be clean but covered. His first problem was what to do with the body. He did not own a car, so he had no means of removing it from the house. He opted for a hiding place within his flat: under the floorboards in his bedroom. And that is where the body remained for eight months, bandaged in plastic sheets, until August 11, 1979. When interviewed by the police, he remarked how amazed he was to discover that the body had decomposed scarcely at all between December, 1978, and August, 1979.

As soon as it was dark on the night of August 11, he had dragged the body to the bottom of the garden, where he had built a huge bonfire, and deposited the corpse in the middle of it. He also added rubber to mask the smell of burning flesh. That victim was never identified.

Nilsen's second victim was a Canadian, Kenneth James Ockenden, aged twenty-three, who was on a touring holiday. They met by chance early in December, 1979, in the *Princess Louise* pub in High Holborn. Nilsen asked him where he would be staying the night and Ockenden replied that he had an aunt and uncle in Carshalton and that is where he intended going: he had already been to the Lake District. Nilsen said that he could sleep at his place and, because it was late, Ockenden accepted the offer. Ockenden was not a homosexual, and there was no sexual attraction between them.

On the way back, they spent £20 on alcohol. While Nilsen cooked ham, eggs and chips, Ockenden watched television and, at the same time, listened through earphones to rock music on the hi-fi system. Not once did he remove these headphones. He ate his meal while still listening to the music and wasn't interested in making conversation.

'All I wanted to do was talk,' Nilsen told detectives. 'I thought to myself: "What a bloody good guest he's turned out to be!" I was livid.' To Nilsen, this was another kind of rejection. Ockenden was strangled with a section of flex, while he sat in a chair, his head full of music.

This time Nilsen was unable to manipulate the body into a groove under the floorboards because of rigor mortis, so he left it covered under the bed for several days, before cutting it up. Then the pieces of flesh and bone were assembled neatly under the floorboards, where his first victim had been kept.

Ockenden had been carrying a large amount of money on him: Nilsen set fire to this after tearing it up. Stealing was a crime and Nilsen was no thief. He prided himself on his honesty.

Victim Number Three was a sixteen-year-old butcher, Martyn Duffey, who died in a similar fashion to the others, while he was drunk. Nilsen was to tell the police: 'It just happened. When I sobered up in the morning, he was dead on the floor. I don't remember how, or why, it happened. By then, I couldn't stop it. I knew it would happen again, sometime, but I didn't have a say in it anymore. Someone else, or something else, was controlling me.'

And so it went on, each new killing very similar to the previous one; a catalogue of casual meetings, followed by equally casual murder and cover-up. Some of the bodies were left around the rooms for several days before being hidden. Chunks of human meat were stored in a brick tomb in the garden shed, which was sprayed every day by Nilsen with a strong-smelling air-freshener. When he burned another victim on a bonfire, he used the opportunity to dispose of other flesh. Much of the killing became a blur for him. Some of the details were precise, others were very vague. He began to kill with only a hazy recollection of what he was doing and the reasons for his actions. Before leaving Melrose Avenue in October, 1981, he destroyed on yet another bonfire all the remaining evidence of his murderous activities.

Nilsen's first victim at No. 23, Cranley Gardens, was boiled in a large, black pot after being hacked into scores of separate pieces. The parts of one man were locked in a tea-chest, while the rest was flushed down the toilet. The head of the final victim was cut off and boiled in the big, black pot. While it was boiling, Nilsen took Bleep for a brisk walk.

When Nilsen's trial began at the Old Bailey on October 24, 1983, he was charged with six murders and two attempted killings. The defence argued that the murder charges should be reduced to manslaughter on the grounds of diminished responsibility, but Nilsen was against being judged insane and, on that score, he won the day.

On Friday, November 4, 1983, Nilsen was found guilty of all the murder charges and was given a 'life' prison sentence. It is worth noting that the jury were not in unanimous agreement: it was a 10-2 majority verdict.

In prison, Nilsen became a prolific writer, describing himself as a 'creative psychopath' who degenerated into a 'destructive psychopath' when he was drunk. He also revealed that after bathing and drying the bodies, he would powder them and himself all over. 'I also wanted to look like a corpse,' he disclosed. 'It is hard to know why I did all these things. I derived no pleasure from killing people, not as far as I can recall. I enjoyed cleaning them afterwards, though, scrubbing off all the dirt of their grubby lives. I have always been a loner, but I wanted to love and to be loved.'

The shed at the bottom of the garden of No. 195, Melrose Avenue was just like any other outdoor storehouse. There were spades, a couple of digging forks, hedge-clippers and a non-motor lawn mower, plus the type of tools that come in handy for home repairs. A fusty smell dominated my nose. In one corner were a few bricks, probably remnants of the makeshift structure in which parts of bodies had been entombed. How could such horror have been enacted amid all this domestic, suburban ordinariness? The taciturn nature of the area and its residents, the sheer respectability of the neighbourhood, only heightened the sense of outrage. The enormity of the crimes was further magnified by the urbane docility of the murderer; a civil servant and a former policeman.

I stood where the bonfires had burned. No smell now. Most of the ash had been scattered by the varying winds of the different seasons. Some of it remained, though, having become a prisoner of the clinging top soil.

Perhaps the neighbours had complained among themselves on those nights when the Guys on the bonfires had not been dummies. The acrid smell, a combination of flesh and rubber, must have filled the night air with an unwholesome miasma, carried for several hundred yards on a steady, prevailing west wind.

However, no one had knocked on Nilsen's door to complain. Tolerance, preserved by the stoical stiff upper lip, was a strong feature of Nilsen's milieu.

New wallpaper, paint and furniture have changed the look of a monument that forever will be a memorial to so many young men who died in their prime for no better reason than it suited Nilsen's whim.

There is a high turnover of residents in both Melrose Avenue and Cranley Gardens. Each new year and every fresh face helps to push Nilsen and his houses of horror further back into oblivion, but total extinction is impossible. He, and others like him, will always be there to haunt the present, just as much as he did the past. The saying that *you never really know what goes on behind closed doors* is probably more applicable to the Dennis Nilsen case than any other.

However, when you make a study of murder, you soon discover that as one door closes, another immediately opens.

Index